Survival Guide for Coaching Youth Basketball

Keith Miniscalco
Greg Kot

Human Kinetics

Library of Congress Cataloging-in-Publication Data

Miniscalco, Keith, 1962-
  Survival guide for coaching youth basketball / Keith Miniscalco, Greg Kot.
    p. cm.
  ISBN-13: 978-0-7360-7383-7 (soft cover)
  ISBN-10: 0-7360-7383-3 (soft cover)
  1. Basketball for children--Coaching. I. Kot, Greg. II. Title.
  GV886.25.M56 2008
  796.32307'7--dc22

                              2008022557

ISBN-10: 0-7360-7383-3 (print)   ISBN-10: 0-7360-7937-8 (Mobipocket)
ISBN-13: 978-0-7360-7383-7 (print)   ISBN-13: 978-0-7360-7937-2 (Mobipocket)

ISBN-10: 0-7360-8111-9 (Adobe PDF)   ISBN-10: 0-7360-7938-6 (Kindle)
ISBN-13: 978-0-7360-8111-5 (Adobe PDF) ISBN-13: 978-0-7360-7938-9 (Kindle)

Acquisitions Editor: Justin Klug; **Developmental Editor:** Heather Healy; **Assistant Editor:** Carla Zych; **Copyeditor:** Jacqueline Eaton Blakley; **Proofreader:** Red Inc.; **Graphic Designer:** Nancy Rasmus; **Graphic Artist:** Tara Welsch; **Cover Designer:** Keith Blomberg; **Photographer (interior):** Neil Bernstein; **Visual Production Assistant:** Joyce Brumfield; **Photo Office Assistant:** Jason Allen; **Art Manager:** Kelly Hendren; **Associate Art Manager:** Alan L. Wilborn; **Illustrator:** Tim Brummett; **Printer:** Sheridan Books

We thank Frank Clark at Oriole Park in Chicago, Illinois, for assistance in providing the location for the photo shoot for this book.

Human Kinetics books are available at special discounts for bulk purchase. Special editions or book excerpts can also be created to specification. For details, contact the Special Sales Manager at Human Kinetics.

Printed in the United States of America   10 9 8 7 6 5 4

The paper in this book is certified under a sustainable forestry program.

Human Kinetics
Web site: www.HumanKinetics.com

United States: Human Kinetics
P.O. Box 5076
Champaign, IL 61825-5076
800-747-4457
e-mail: humank@hkusa.com

Canada: Human Kinetics
475 Devonshire Road, Unit 100
Windsor, ON N8Y 2L5
800-465-7301 (in Canada only)
e-mail: info@hkcanada.com

Europe: Human Kinetics
107 Bradford Road
Stanningley
Leeds LS28 6AT, United Kingdom
+44 (0)113 255 5665
e-mail: hk@hkeurope.com

Australia: Human Kinetics
57A Price Avenue
Lower Mitcham, South Australia 5062
08 8372 0999
e-mail: info@hkaustralia.com

New Zealand: Human Kinetics
P.O. Box 80
Torrens Park, South Australia 5062
0800 222 062
e-mail: info@hknewzealand.com

For Liz and Deb, who are always there for us—win or lose.

 # Contents

Drill Finder   vii
Preface   ix
Acknowledgments   xi
Key to Diagrams   xiii

1 Help! Where Do I Start?   1

2 Organizing Your Team Practices   19

3 Developing Offensive Skills With 10 Simple Drills   39

4 Teaching Defensive Skills With 10 Simple Drills   77

5 Your Can't-Miss Offensive Playbook   103

6 Surefire Defensive Sets   125

7 Special Plays and Situations   137

8 Game Time! What's My Role Again?   157

About the Authors   169

Drill Finder

Drill title	Skill level			Skills					Page no.
	Beg.	Int.	Adv.	Passing	Dribbling	Shooting	Rebounding	Defensive skills	
Knockout	✔					✔			34
Two-player passing	✔			✔					35
Three-man weave		✔		✔					36
Hand speed stationary dribbling	✔	✔	✔		✔				58
Dribbling	✔				✔				62
Circle up	✔					✔			64
Pivoting	✔			✔	✔	✔	✔		65
Step and square	✔	✔				✔			66
Lay ups	✔	✔	✔			✔			68
Give-and-go		✔		✔		✔			70
Basket cutting		✔		✔		✔			72
Two balls on the block		✔				✔	✔		73
Screen and roll			✔	✔		✔			74
Ready, set, defense	✔							✔	88
Z slides	✔							✔	89
Close-outs	✔							✔	90
Foot-fire	✔							✔	91
Sky high	✔		✔				✔	✔	92
Wing deny		✔						✔	94
Help defense		✔						✔	95
Tandem defense		✔						✔	96
Cut the cutter		✔						✔	98
Shell			✔					✔	99

 # Preface

You've got a bag of basketballs, a clipboard, and a whistle. You walk into a gym full of squirming eight- and nine-year-olds whose basketball IQ begins and ends with the knowledge that a team scores points by putting an orange ball into a hoop. Your assignment: Turn this eager but disorganized gang of neophytes into a team, preferably before your first game. And, oh, by the way, the first game is two weeks away.

The start of the season can be a nerve-racking time for a new coach. *Where do I start? What positions do these kids play? How much playing time do I give each player? What if they don't pay attention? What if we lose? What will the parents think? What if the kids are embarrassed? What if I'm embarrassed?* If you are a first-time coach wondering what you've gotten yourself into, relax—we're here to help you.

Survival Guide for Coaching Youth Basketball is aimed at first-time coaches and the 5- to 10-year-old boys and girls on their teams, as well as their parents. It provides a quick, clear, fun way of teaching fundamental basketball skills that will serve your kids for a lifetime. This book will help the first-time coach

- provide age-appropriate instruction during practices,
- maximize practice time with fun games and the best drills for skill development,
- evaluate players to determine realistic goals,
- provide proven offensive plays and defensive schemes that younger players can run,
- teach during games, and
- show young athletes why and how they can be more effective playing as a team than as individuals.

The days leading up to that first game are an exciting and anxious time for coaches and their teams. This book is designed to ease the pressure and give you the confidence to walk into your first practice and each practice thereafter knowing you'll accomplish something. It will map out an entire season of quick, simple drills and strategies. As your players become familiar with the concepts in this book, they will begin to realize that what they learn in practice mirrors what they do in real basketball games. They will begin applying the practice fundamentals in game situations.

Coaching is a process, and so is learning. You don't have much time to impart knowledge with only a practice or two a week, but you also need to be patient. So being organized and efficient will help you maximize your practice time. Setting realistic goals and knowing when to raise or lower the bar of expectations will give your players the best learning environment. Knowing what to teach and when, and using drills the youngsters can understand and accomplish, will be key to surviving your first season as a coach. This book will take you step by step through the process of creating a structure for your practices, games, and season.

In the following chapters, you will find easy-to-understand drills, defensive concepts, and offensive fundamentals that you can teach and begin implementing in your very first practice. The book will also help you organize and run a practice down to the minute, because spending too much time on a particular drill can be nearly as detrimental as not spending enough.

If it's all about winning, this book is not for you. The outcome of a game between eight-year-olds should not matter, though winning is always a nice bonus. Above all, the kids should have fun while building a foundation for playing basketball that will serve them well as they grow into the game. This book is about learning to play basketball the right way. It's about learning to love the game and learning how to become part of something bigger than the individual: a team. If young athletes learn that, they'll all be winners sooner or later. This book will help coaches start young athletes down that winning path.

⦿ Acknowledgments

A coach never stops learning. We have many teachers we'd like to thank for showing us the way: Coaches Tanya Johnson, Mary Just, Colleen Chipman, and Dick Baumgartner foremost among them. We have also benefited from the advice and friendship of our fellow coaches in the Over the Edge traveling basketball program, especially Marty Gaughan, Kevin Gleason, and Kandace Lenti.

This book would not be possible without the input of our many friends at Human Kinetics, especially Brian Holding, who initiated this idea and was our advocate from the start; Jason Muzinic and Justin Klug, who helped us shape and refine the concept and made sure everything stayed on course; and Heather Healy, who spent many long hours editing (and improving) the manuscript.

The photo shoot went off without a hitch in large measure due to the professionalism and welcoming nature of photographer Neil Bernstein and acquisitions editor Justin Klug. The young athletes and their families were equally patient and in good spirits, and we are indebted to them. Thanks to Pat, Joanne, Jeffery, and Jabarie McCoy; Kevin, Kelly, Margaret, Grace, and Kathleen Gleason; Marty, Mary, and Danny Gaughan; James, Deb, and Ntsang Atanga' McCormick; and Mark, Diane, and Peter Muench. We would especially like to thank Steve and Susan Besch, and their daughter Kayla, for their assistance during the photo session.

There's only one way to "research" a book like this, and that's to spend many hours in the gym. Our families have been beyond patient in putting up with our passion for the game. Our daughters—Caitlin, Brenna, and Kelly Miniscalco, and Katie and Marissa Kot—shared many of those hours in the gym with us, and yet continue to lead happy and productive lives. We couldn't be prouder of them.

Keith Miniscalco and Greg Kot
Chicago, 2008

Key to Diagrams

	Offensive player
	Defensive player
	Offensive player who starts with ball
	Defensive player who starts with ball
	Player relocates to this position
$\longrightarrow$	Path of player
$----\blacktriangleright$	Path of ball
$\longrightarrow\!\!\!\dashv$	Screen
$\sim\!\!\sim\!\!\sim\!\!\blacktriangleright$	Dribble
	Pivot
	Coach

Help!
Where Do I Start?

Coaching beginner youth basketball is a lot like trying to bottle lightning. You enter a gym containing a dozen eager would-be hoops stars, tasked with channeling their energy into a team sport that demands discipline, athleticism, patience, speed, unselfishness, and brains. But right now, you're just trying to figure out how to make this scene look a little less like Romper Room.

The kids are bouncing basketballs off the floor, off the walls, and off each other. They are running around as though being chased by a huge invisible Rottweiler. They have a general idea how to play the game (the orange ball goes in the basket), but that's about it. You are a lot more savvy than they are in playing the game, but you don't have a lot of experience coaching it. You're a volunteer, the designated parent—the guy or gal who might've played a little ball in school and some pickup games in the driveway and then raised your hand when the park supervisor or school athletic director asked for a little help coaching basketball this season.

Now you've just walked into the gym and reality hits: it's your job to turn this unruly little mob of mischief makers into a team during the course of the season. And, oh yeah, smile while you're doing it! What have you just gotten yourself into? Could somebody have made a mistake? Will you need therapy afterward? However you came into coaching the game, you need to get organized, and quickly.

This book is designed to help you, the rookie coach, learn how to help kids ages 5 to 10 play the game of basketball. As any beginner coach quickly realizes, it's one thing to know how to play the game, and quite another to know how to teach it. A talented athlete performs almost by instinct; years of training reinforce muscle memory, allowing a basketball player to compete with quick reactions and anticipation.

But beginner athletes aren't so fortunate. They need to learn basic aspects of the game that the older athlete takes for granted—dribbling, shooting, passing, even catching the ball. And their exposure to team sports is often minimal. They need to learn not only how to play the game but how to work with other beginners toward a common goal. Beginner athletes may not appreciate any of this. Your biggest challenge may be just getting the kids to quiet down long enough so you can actually string together two or three sentences before the chatterboxes go back to doing what they do best: making a whole lot of noise.

The task of coaching youth basketball may seem daunting, but it's actually a lot of fun. Catch kids at an early enough age, and they're like little sponges—ready to absorb just about anything from anyone who looks like they know what they're talking about. So a new coach can have an immediate impact.

Any would-be athlete, no matter how talented, needs to learn the fundamentals to play the game well. Bad habits—faulty footwork, dicey shooting technique, sloppy dribbling—start at an early age and become more difficult to break as the players get older. The younger and more inexperienced the player, the more quickly those bad habits can be undone and replaced with sound techniques that can endure through a lifetime of basketball games. A coach can make a difference in a young player's life by teaching the fundamentals and imparting the values of working hard; working together; and working with coaches, teammates, opponents, and referees—as well as the values of the game itself.

And that's where this book comes in. Lots of books are aimed at developing players who already have the fundamentals and have been playing for years. But what about the player who doesn't even know what the fundamentals are? Lots of kids try to play basketball at the junior high or high school levels without the proper foundation, only to find themselves sitting on the bench or getting cut from the team altogether. They may know how to put the ball in the basket, but they can't dribble with their off hand, they travel every time they try to pivot, and they consistently get beat on defense. Here's the book those kids and their coaches could've used when they were just starting out.

Furthermore, this book is designed to help new coaches build not just solid basketball players, but fundamentally sound teams. All players, no matter their skill level, can be an asset to the team by learning how to play the game the right way. Your goal, as a coach, is to have each member of your team contribute. This leads to a positive experience for everyone on the roster, including the person in charge. So let's get started.

Learning the Basics

Before even stepping foot in a gym with a new team, the rookie coach needs to have a few things organized. These basics cover everything from having the proper equipment to being prepared for a medical emergency. It can involve knowing what hours the gym is available, how to turn on the lights once you get there, and what to have in your gym bag to make sure every practice runs smoothly. It's easy to lose track of such details while preparing for a new season, so this chapter can serve as a checklist of preseason and early-season must-dos.

Know the Gym

Before the season starts, get a sense of where you'll be practicing and playing games, and assess the layout of the gym so you can plan your workouts accordingly. Try to visit the facility ahead of time so there won't be any surprises. Note the dimensions of the court: Is it regulation size? Does it have all the proper markings for baseline, sideline, free-throw line, midcourt, and so on? And note the number of baskets (most courts will have at least two, but some may have as many as six).

Find out whether the baskets are height adjustable to accommodate younger, smaller players who are just starting to learn the game. Will you need a key to access the gym? Where are the light switches? Whom at the facility should be contacted if there is a cancellation? Is there a storage room onsite with basketballs? Is it locked? Or will you need to bring basketballs?

Be sure you'll have access to the following equipment at your first practice:

- **Basketballs.** Ball size can be important, especially for younger players with smaller hands. A smaller ball is easier to handle and allows players to form good ballhandling skills and sound shooting mechanics. Most leagues or tournaments use a 28.5-inch ball for girls and all younger players, and a 29.5-inch ball for boys fifth grade and up.

   If your league or gym provides basketballs, you're all set. But if not, you'll need to buy basketballs and a mesh bag or large gym bag to carry them. (Another option is to ask players to bring their own ball to practice, but coaches should always bring at least one or two of their own basketballs). Ideally, each player on the team should have a ball for individual ballhandling drills, but basketballs can be expensive, so try to have at least one ball for every two players; if you have a 12-person roster, you will need a minimum of 6 basketballs. Special basketballs for shooting mechanics are available. These basketballs use hand prints and positioning lines on the ball to help form a proper shot.

The more basketballs you have, the less waiting around players will do during practice. Always carry basketballs in your car, and bring at least two balls to every game—you will need them for warm-ups, and some leagues require you to bring your own to play the game.

- **Pullovers or pinnies.** Pullovers will allow you to distinguish between two teams when you are setting up offenses and defenses during practice. They can also be used in games as an alternative to the regular uniform top if the two teams have similar-colored uniforms. Pullovers can be bought in any sports store in a variety of colors. You will need to have five on hand so you can match up teams in full- and half-court five-on-five drills and competition.

- **First-aid kit.** Some leagues may have kits on hand at the scorer's table during games, but don't count on it. It's even rarer to have an athletic trainer or medical professional available in case of injury to one of the players (or, in certain instances, the coach who suddenly finds himself with a splitting migraine). So it's always good to be prepared. Coaching kits containing tape, bandages, instant cold packs, and other quickie medical gear can be readily ordered on the Internet. It's amazing how much time you can waste in a practice or a game hunting for a bandage or ice pack. This way, it's all in one box, and you can fix up players in no time and get them back into action. Whether you're using a league kit or providing your own, you'll need to add at least two more items for yourself. These items will be your most valuable assistant coaches: aspirin and patience. Without them, it could be a long season.

- **Dry-erase board and markers.** These tools can be used in practice or games to draw up positions for defense and offense and to show rotation in play sets for offense and defense. Dry-erase boards are easy to use and reuse, and they sure beat messy pen and paper. Most leagues will not provide boards or markers, so plan on purchasing these items yourself.

Be aware that your players may be tempted to use the board as an impromptu art project while they're sitting on the bench, which may dry out your pens sooner than expected. Prevent a catastrophe: pack an extra dry-erase marker for each game. Better yet, pack two. For the coach, there's nothing more frustrating than running out of ink while drawing up another genius, game-winning play.

Now that you have your gear lined up, you need to get familiar with the practice facility. If you are in a league or working with a school team, practice time and a gym are usually provided. How much time you have to practice can vary widely. There's never enough. The key is to make the most of what's available. To organize your practice sessions, you'll need to know the following:

- **Where are the bathrooms?** The answer to this question may perhaps be the most important of all. You will face this question early and often, so you'd better have the answer from the first minute of the first practice.

- **How much practice time will be allowed?** (How many practices a week? How many minutes per practice?) At minimum, you'd like to have two 60-minute practices a week, but you may have to settle for less. During the height of basketball season, gym time can be a precious commodity, and younger teams are usually at the end of the priority list. If this is the case, make the most of what you have.

  One practice a week can still be productive, especially if it lays the groundwork for additional practice at home, away from the team. This may require the coach to have a frank discussion with the parents: "Look, I can show the kids what they need to know once or twice a week in practice. But for them to improve, they're going to need to work on some of these things at home, on their own. So I'm enlisting your help in making some of these drills part of your child's daily routine." If that doesn't work, don't sweat it. Just do the best you can with what you have, keep things simple, and build up skill training slowly over the course of the season. Remember, you're running a marathon with these kids, not a sprint.

- **How much of the court can you use?** In most cases, you'll have the run of the entire court. This is ideal because the team will acclimate themselves to game conditions more rapidly. But if the court is not regulation size or has only one usable basket, you will have to adjust accordingly. If you are splitting the court with another team, you will have to work at one basket. But it's nothing to stress about. Most drills described in this book can be accomplished on just about any court of just about any size or at a single basket.

- **How many baskets do you get to use?** A single court can have as many as six goals. If you have additional baskets, you can split the team into groups and have them working on a drill simultaneously. This will enable you to speed up practice and get through many more drills in the allotted time. In general, the bigger your roster, the better it is to have more baskets. But working with the entire team on a single basket also has advantages, because you can watch and instruct one group at a time and be heard by everyone on the team. Do not be discouraged by any situation. If you have a ball and a basket, you can teach a lot of basketball.

Ideally, you'll want to practice on an official court with the lines marked: baselines, sidelines, half-court line, free-throw lines and free-throw lane lines, and three-point lines (see figure 1.1). That way, the players will already be comfortable with the court layout when they start playing games.

Beginner players who have practiced using only one basket can get confused when confronted with double the scoring opportunity during the actual game. If you manage to go through an entire season without your team scoring at least a basket or two for the other team because of confusion about which basket is which, consider yourself fortunate.

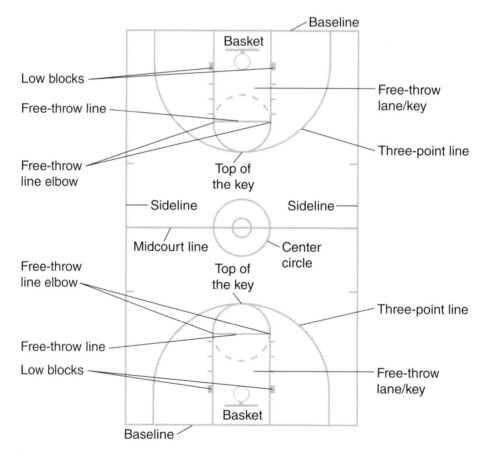

Figure 1.1   Basketball court with proper line markings.

Also note that players may need to be reminded several times during a game which basket they are defending. A coach working with players in this age group should take nothing for granted.

Check to see whether the baskets can be lowered. Many new facilities have baskets that can be adjusted for younger players. Lowering baskets from 10 feet to 8 feet can help develop good shooting mechanics and allow the younger players to have a more realistic basketball experience.

Know the Rules

League and tournament rules will vary according to age and local custom, and you need to know them so you can adjust your practice and game plan accordingly. Here are the questions you'll need to have answered before the game starts.

- **How long are the games?** Playing time may be divided into four quarters or two halves. You'll need to find out the length of time for each period; it will vary for age level. Halves are often 16 to 18 minutes long, while quarters are often 5 to 7 minutes long. You'll need to find out if the clock runs continuously or if it stops every time a referee blows the whistle for free throws, fouls, etc. The length and speed of the games will affect your decisions about individual playing time and substitutions.

- **How many fouls until bonus free throws are shot?** In some leagues, a team is allowed six fouls per half without additional penalty; on the seventh foul, free throws are awarded even for nonshooting fouls. Once a tenth foul is committed, the free-throw shooter is awarded two shots for all fouls.

   But the rules can vary. In some leagues, the let-them-play philosophy prevails and fouls are rarely called. Other leagues may not keep track of individual or team fouls. Sometimes this is done to ensure that the games finish on time, especially if other later games are scheduled. Whatever the case, you need to be aware of the rules so that you can run the team accordingly. And players need to be made aware of how fouls affect a game and their individual playing time, starting in practice when defensive skills are emphasized.

- **How many time-outs are allowed per game?** Two per half? Three per game? More? The more time-outs you have, the better you are able to manage the game and instruct the players. If you have fewer time-outs, you will have to prepare the players accordingly in practices leading up to games and perhaps simplify your strategy.

- **Are teams allowed to full-court press on defense?** Sometimes a press is permitted only at the end of each half or at the end of a game. In most beginner leagues, pressing is not allowed at all. If you face the possibility of being pressed by the opposing team, you will need to prepare for this at practice.

- **Is each team responsible for providing a scorekeeper?** In many tournaments and leagues, each team must provide a volunteer to assist with keeping the official scorebook or running the scoreboard. Usually, the coach can call on a parent, some of whom will instantly run for cover and protest that they've never done anything like this before. With a broad, welcoming smile, the rookie coach can authoritatively assure the fearful volunteer that it's not as difficult as it looks. Usually, one of the referees will know how to operate the scoreboard and can instruct the volunteer in a matter of minutes. The scorebook volunteer needs only to keep track of individual scoring and fouls. The referees will call out the number of each player as the individual commits the foul, which is then checked off next to the player's name and number in the scorebook.

Additionally, some traditional rules may be left out or overlooked to help young players as they learn the game. At the youngest age levels, these rules sometimes can be adjusted by mutual consent of the opposing coaches and referees. At other times, the referees may inform the coaches of the adjustments before the game. Rules that may be ignored or bent include the following:

- **Traveling.** Referees may allow younger players to take several steps while trying to dribble the basketball.
- **Double dribble.** The ballhandler may be allowed to stop and start the dribble again.
- **Free throws.** The free-throw line may be moved up to help young shooters reach the basket.

Heading Off Problems

Coaches will quickly find that they must play many roles to have a successful team. In addition to coaching the fundamentals of a great game, they are part-time parents, guidance counselors, parental advisers, medical assistants, and, occasionally, miracle workers. Keep the focus on the best interests of the players, and things will usually work out well. But you will also need to be prepared when things don't go according to plan. Players will get hurt. Parents will become disgruntled. Snacks will be forgotten. These are situations that require coaches to be on their game.

Protect Yourself and Your Players

Leagues and tournaments routinely require players to provide proof of insurance and waiver forms for injuries. It is also a good idea to have medical cards like the one shown in figure 1.2 (on page 10) filled out for any medical emergencies that may arise. These cards should include emergency phone numbers, doctors' numbers, and medication guidelines, and should be kept with your first-aid kit so they are handy at practices and games.

Most accidents happen in practice, when there are no other adults around. So a coach must have some type of first-aid training to prepare for medical emergencies. A CPR class is also highly recommended. A doctor you are not, but in many instances you are the first responder. You should always have a cell phone handy to call 911 in an emergency.

For more routine injuries, a coach with a combination of first-aid training and common sense can make a huge difference. For bloody noses, for example, have the player sit down and lean forward, and pinch the bridge of the nose to control the bleeding. For a twisted ankle, remove the injured player's shoe and have the injured player lie down; ice the injury immediately and elevate the ankle above the head to prevent swelling. Besides cuts, bruises, black eyes, bloody noses, and sprained ankles, you need to become familiar with relatively common medical conditions such as diabetes and asthma. You'll need to recognize the signs of distress and how to deal with them.

Above all, protect the kids from themselves. Basketball is a contact sport, and it can encourage roughhousing, wrestling, ball throwing, trash talking, and general mayhem. For those athletes who just can't seem to control all their energy in practice, find a productive outlet to burn it off. Have the more overzealous kids run a few laps around the gym while you continue practicing with the rest of the team. Not only will this reduce their energy for rabble-rousing, it'll get them in shape to sprint up and down the floor during games.

Involve the Parents

Parents can and should be a coach's best allies. Get them on your side from the get-go by scheduling a parents-only meeting with them before the season begins. Begin by offering all your contact info: home phone, work phone, cell phone, e-mail. Suggest when the best times are to reach

Figure 1.2   Sample Medical Card

Athlete's Name _____ Age _____

Parents' or Guardians' Contact Information

Name _____

Address _____ Home phone _____

Mother's or guardian's work phone _____ Mobile phone _____

Father's or guardian's work phone _____ Mobile phone _____

Emergency Contact (if parents cannot be reached)

Name _____ Phone _____

Medical Information

Allergies _____

Medical conditions _____

Doctor's name _____ Phone _____

Authorization for Medical Treatment

The undersigned grants permission to the coach in charge to authorize emergency treatment considered necessary by qualified medical personnel for the athlete whose name appears below. It is understood that every effort will be made to contact parents immediately when an emergency occurs.

Name of athlete _____

Father's or guardian's signature _____

Mother's or guardian's signature _____

you. In addition, obtain all their relevant information. Then get into the nitty-gritty of what you expect from your players and what they should expect from you. Finally, ask the parents for their questions.

Among the key issues are certain to be playing time (you'll want to keep playing time as equal as possible for all players), practice and game schedules (where, when, how often), and team goals (fundamental skills development versus winning). Let the parents know that you will need their help in running the team: they will need to transport their kids to practices and games and may want to form carpools; they may need to help with scorekeeping at games; and they will be asked to encourage their children to practice at home.

Some parents will be gung ho and ask to help out in any way possible. Some may even offer to become your assistants (not a bad idea, as long as it's clear you're in charge). Others will walk out of the meeting and never be heard from again, content not to have any input into their child's activities. No matter what their attitude, it's important for the coach to stay in touch regularly with the parents, usually via a team e-mail in which you can address the progress of the players and the upcoming schedule of games and practices.

Touch base with parents individually as the need arises, whether it's for a medical or disciplinary issue or to praise a player who is exceeding expectations. Assure the parents that they should come to you to resolve any issues that arise before those issues turn into problems. Better to communicate a little too much rather than not enough. At least parents will know that you care and have their child's best interests at heart.

If problems do arise, they should be handled off the court, never in front of other families or the athletes themselves. Parents should not approach you at a game if they have a problem with something that happened on the court. Both parties need to cool off before having a discussion. If parents insist on addressing the issue immediately, assure them that now is not the right time and that you will contact them the next day. At this point, you really are on public display, and how you handle yourself will tell the other parents a lot about your character. This would not be a good time to become defensive, self-righteous, angry, loud, combative, confrontational, threatening, or even mildly irritated. Above all, you need to be cool and professional, even if the parent isn't.

Such unpleasantness can sometimes be avoided by being preemptive. Address issues about playing time and which positions the kids will play at the informal parents' meeting before the season even starts. When all else fails, keep your able assistants—patience and aspirin—close at all times, and remember that it's about the kids, not your ego.

Parents generally like to know about games and practices as far ahead of time as possible so they can plan their schedules accordingly. Strive to maintain a regular practice schedule—such as 5 p.m. on Tuesdays and Thursdays—and stick to it. If this is not possible, inform parents about why and strive to provide them with information as soon as it becomes available. Any exceptions to the schedule due to work conflicts or illness should be addressed as far ahead of time as possible. Nothing promotes chaos in a household more readily than a last-minute schedule change. If the coach stays on top of this situation and is considerate of parents' schedules, it'll be a huge plus for coach–parent relations.

For younger teams, a snack schedule is a must. Many times, it is a league rule to provide snacks for the players after a game. If so, bring a signup sheet for parents to the meeting. Keep the snacks light and portable so the players can pick them up and go if they have to dash off right after the game. Also, it's a good idea to keep a stash of goodies in your car in case a parent forgets. Losing a game can be a tough blow for a kid's ego, but a loss is not nearly as devastating as going snackless after a hard-fought game.

Enlist the parents to make sure the players take pride in their appearance. It's a reflection not only of the player but of the entire team, and paying attention to this issue sends a message to the players to respect the game. Proper practice and game attire are about looking good, but they're also about playing safely and comfortably. Proper equipment should be worn: basketball shoes (not running shoes), socks, basketball shorts, T-shirt, and especially kneepads. Require your players to wear kneepads, even if the league or tournament you play in does not.

Players generally don't like to wear kneepads. But they're as essential in youth basketball as batting helmets in youth baseball. Wearing them can prevent serious injury. A knee injury at this early stage of a child's development can lead to permanent health issues that could easily have been averted. Of more immediate concern, any type of injury can severely limit playing time. An injury to a sensitive body part such as the knee can also discourage a player from playing at a high level of intensity for fear of reinjury.

No jewelry of any kind should be worn. That means no earrings, watches, rings, or hair clips. Players should keep their hair out of their faces. In lieu of a haircut, players should wear a headband or athletic prewrap. Additionally, during games players should always tuck in their shirts and double-knot their shoelaces. To drive home the point, apply these dress codes in practice as well. The kids may complain, but they'll learn they need to be prepared.

Every player should come to practices and games with their own easily identified water bottle. Water should be consumed slowly but frequently during games and practices; save the sport drinks for before and after competition. Keeping your athletes hydrated is extremely important, and frequent water breaks during a hard practice are a must. Remember to pack a bottle for yourself, too.

Defining Your Coaching Philosophy

At its simplest, coaching basketball helps provide a positive, healthy, fun outlet for kids. At its most demanding, coaching basketball allows you to help shape the basketball players of tomorrow. Even Michael Jordan didn't have a clue how to play the game at one point. Someone had to coach him.

Be sure, though, to keep your expectations in check: the next Michael Jordan is probably not playing on your team. You're coaching beginner or, at best, novice basketball. Many of these kids won't even play high school basketball for the varsity, let alone get college scholarships or go pro.

So define your role. You are a teacher, and at its most basic, your job is to teach the fundamentals of the game. Teach individual skills and develop them. Teach respect for the game and discipline. Crack a joke or two while doing it—that'll keep the kids laughing as they learn and prevent the veins in your neck from exploding like blasting caps.

Along the way, larger lessons can be taught and absorbed. Winning should not be your top priority. Winning is a bonus. These young athletes have to feel good about their experience. They have to have fun! And how do you make that happen? Have a sense of humor about yourself and your players. Enjoy them for who they are, and don't criticize them for what they are not. Make each player feel like she has a stake in the team. Rotate responsibilities, and make a point of singling out each player on the team at some point during practice to commend a good play, an exciting move, or a heady response to one of your coaching points. When making one of those coaching points, don't tell, ask! Before you jump in, give the players a chance to make your point for you by asking them how they would handle a particular situation.

If you have organization and structure in your program, you will be successful no matter the number of wins or losses. Sportsmanship—how to win gracefully and lose with dignity—is a lesson that every player can take away from his experience, no matter what the skill level.

In learning the game of basketball, the kids are also learning about life. They see firsthand how working together enables them to accomplish a common goal and how hard work, discipline, and persistence can lead to better results, individually and collectively. They discover how to overcome obstacles to reach a higher objective. They learn that not everything in life results in victory and that many worthwhile accomplishments require effort, even struggle.

Coaches are guides in this discovery process. It can be difficult for players and coaches to smile through all of it; we've all seen kids (and even a few coaches!) cry after a tough loss. But the smart coach recognizes that a defeat is not a failure, it's a teaching opportunity—a way to measure how far the team has come and decide what the coach and players need to do to travel the next distance.

Let parents and players know about your coaching goals upfront. The idea is to make clear to everyone, including yourself, what you are doing and why. Setting certain goals for the team can be an effective way of communicating this to everyone. The idea is to start slow and finish the season strong. Keep the goals realistic based on the team's skill level and age. Maybe the goal for the beginner team is to aim to score double-digit points in each of the last two games. Or that each child scores a point, or at least takes a shot that hits the rim by the end of the season. Or that all players take at least three dribbles toward the basket with their nondominant hand during a game.

Each achieved goal deserves some sort of celebration, whether it's a high five from everyone on the team or postgame ice cream. A pat on the back will show the kids that what they do is being noticed and appreciated, and a coach can't do that enough. In doing so, the coach sets up her team for even more success; players who briefly bask in the glow of public acclaim have an incentive to keep improving so they can have that experience again.

Make a point of acknowledging not only the obvious accomplishment (the game-winning basket, the spectacular steal) but also the more subtle ones: the kid who dives on the floor for a loose ball, the little guard who goes up amid the big trees in the lane and battles for a rebound (even if the little guard ends up on his fanny without the ball), or the reluctant shooter who hits the rim with a free throw. Above all, the coach needs to create a positive environment for all the players on the team, not just the stars or the most gifted athletes. This can be accomplished in several ways.

- **Provide equal playing time.** No matter what the outcome of the game, at beginner or novice levels every player needs to participate equally. A team can still compete by playing its better players at strategic intervals—the beginning and end of the game or near the end of the first half. But otherwise, keep rotating your players off and on the floor so that everyone's involved.

- **Rotate positions.** Guards, forwards, and centers should trade jobs throughout the season and in practice to learn the different skills and responsibilities of each position. Yes, give the tallest player on your team a shot at point guard and have your little ballhandler take a turn at center. Your players will appreciate the adventure, and it should give everyone on the team a deeper appreciation of the game.

- **Encourage outside practice.** To really develop, basketball players need to work out on their own. This isn't always possible, and not every player will live in a home that makes such activity possible. But do provide each player with a take-home lesson with the expectation that not every player may be able to complete the assignment. Make it clear to players and parents that this falls under the category of extra credit rather than homework.

- **Promote attendance.** Bear in mind that players sometimes show up late or miss practice through no fault of their own; their parents may have a conflict, the player may be sick, or homework from school may be piling up. All are legitimate excuses and should not be held against the player. But reward the kids who do show up regularly and on time for practice by allowing them to pick favorite drills for everyone to work on at practice. Show them you recognize their dedication without penalizing their teammates who may not be in a position to do the same.

- **Encourage teamwork.** One selfish player can break up the chemistry and camaraderie of any team. Unselfishness leads to easy baskets and lots of wins. Teach your players to pass first, shoot second. Get the ball to the open teammate every time. Players should learn from Day 1 that they need to pass up an open shot if a pass will result in an even better shot for someone else. Sharing the ball makes everyone feel part of the team and is a philosophy that should be reiterated at every practice and during every game.

- **Demonstrate respect for the referees.** Contrary to the trash talk you might hear from the fans, referees are not only human, they usually get the call right. When they get it wrong, we should resist all temptation to land on them like a ton of bricks. Be professional when talking to the officials, because your players will follow your lead. Most referees will answer your question about a call they have made. Yelling and screaming get you nowhere and can even hurt your team. Your behavior can also set an example for parents in the stands.

- **Demonstrate good sportsmanship.** From the start, your players should focus less on what the other team is doing and more on what they and their teammates are doing. The other team is an opponent, not an enemy. Teach your players to respect their opponents. During the game, they can show respect to the other team by playing hard but clean. After the game, they congratulate the other team, win or lose.

The Coach's Clipboard

✔ Make sure you have basketballs, pullovers, a medical kit, and a dry-erase board.

✔ Scope out the layout of the practice gym and adjust practice routine accordingly.

✔ Find out where the bathrooms are!

✔ Know the rules of the league (time-outs, length of each half, etc.).

✔ Gather medical cards and proofs of insurance.

✔ Get the parents involved and keep them informed.

✔ Ensure that each player has proper equipment, especially kneepads.

✔ Don't forget the snacks!

✔ Set team goals and emphasize sportsmanship.

✔ Winning is a bonus, not the be-all and end-all.

Organizing Your Team Practices

Prep time is over. Now you're facing a gym full of hooligans in basketball shorts, all of them up for just about anything that will allow them to scream, shout, jump, run, slide, tackle, or just plain cut loose. Your job is to get them to focus on basketball. So, how do you seize their attention and hold it for the next 60 to 90 minutes? And, no, wearing a clown suit and juggling three basketballs while balancing on a unicycle is not an option.

Running a practice means playing several roles, often at once; besides being a coach, you're a teacher, a disciplinarian, a therapist, a medical assistant, and an emcee. And for any good emcee, it's critical to keep the show moving; the kids (and you) will have a lot more fun that way. Spending too much time on any one drill can be counterproductive, if not an invitation to chaos, as the kids' minds start to wander.

Remember, you're dealing with attention spans shaped by computer mouse clicks and television remotes. If things lack maximum excitement for even a second, zap! Little Johnny or Jenny's mind has left the building in search of the next thrill. The kids can't zap you, but they can mentally tune you out, so beware the wandering eyes, the shuffling feet, the tapping toes, and the unstifled yawns. Here are a couple of quick tips to help you maintain attention.

- **Talk, don't preach.** Save the speeches for your hall of fame induction ceremony. The best practices are about action and participation. Demonstrate a coaching point, let the kids follow suit, then tweak and refine as they perform. Kids learn a lot faster by doing rather than watching, so get everyone involved. In moments of extreme disarray, start over, and try to smile about it. A joke might help.

- **Invoke Socrates.** Yes, Socrates, a man who taught by asking questions. "Now, who can show me the difference between a bounce pass and a chest pass?" Find the one kid who gets it, and let him demonstrate. It's a way of saying to the other kids, "See, it's not that tough." And if the kids are a little sloppy at first, relax. Laugh with them while encouraging them to keep at it with little bits of advice (not a speech). This is a season, not a one-and-done deal, so look at each practice as a building block rather than a project that needs to be finished today.

Surviving the First Practices

In many ways, the first practices are the most stressful for both the coach and the team. Coaches still aren't quite sure what they're getting themselves into, and for the kids it's like the first day at school, full of unanswered questions: *What's the classroom look like? Will my teacher be nice? What's going to be expected of me?* And then there are the kids who show up and think it's playtime, with no expectations of learning anything, just horsing around as much as possible out of earshot of Mom and Dad.

But a coach can quickly ease these doubts and false expectations by getting organized. The key is to go into each practice with a plan and take charge of the situation from the first minute. If the plan doesn't work right down to the second, don't fret. At least you will have a sense of what you want to accomplish at each practice and how. If you get through most of it, you'll have done a lot, and you'll have taught the kids more about basketball than most of them have learned in their entire lives until now. But if you come in disorganized and unsure, that can set the wrong tone for everything that follows. A few minutes of planning can make all the difference between a great practice and a waste of time.

Just as critical as having a plan is having a personality. A coach needs to meet her team halfway, not as a remote authoritarian but as an approachable teacher. You're not their pal, but you are their guide. Your aim is to help the kids learn to enjoy and respect a great game, not buff up your ego with a string of wins on your way to the Youth League Coaches Hall of Fame.

Break the ice with your team at the first practices by getting to know each player by name. By putting their minds at ease about who you are and what you expect, you can pave the way for a fun, productive season. Nobody likes an uptight coach who wants everything done just so from the first day. Strive for improvement, not perfection. Make it clear to the kids—and yourself—that you're there to help them develop whatever talent they have. You're not expecting all of them to be stars, but you are expecting all of them to have a positive, productive experience.

That goes double for the first few practices. You aren't going to mold a great team with a handful of practices. Instead, you're forging a relationship with your team and the individual players that will allow you to achieve success over several months. You're setting a tone and giving the players a sense of who you are and what you expect. You're also getting a sense of who your players are and what they're going to need from you to learn the game. What happens in the first practice will dictate in many ways what happens in the second. You'll begin to understand how much to challenge the kids and how much to nurture them, and then you'll be fine-tuning the balance for the rest of the season.

From the start, instill confidence. Many of the kids will be bewildered when they realize that basketball involves a whole lot more than putting the ball in the hoop. Some will be intimidated by the disparity in talent. A few will be itching for a chance to show off. Let them know right away that it doesn't matter what they do or don't know about the game. What matters is how much they learn, starting today. Hustle is everything. Assure them that if they try hard, everything's going to be fine.

Getting to Know Your Players

Before bouncing any basketballs, introduce yourself and any assistant coaches. Take the kids on a tour of the court to make sure they understand all the lines and markings. This should be done in the form of a question-and-answer walkaround, so the kids and coach are interacting right away. Quiz the kids later in the practice about some of the markings, and offer an extra postgame snack to the player who gets the most correct answers. This is a great way to set the correct tone at practice: Coach is in charge, but the players should always feel welcome to ask a question and interact with the coach.

Then ask all the players to *briefly* introduce themselves: name, favorite food, names of any pets, and favorite school subject (and, no, gym doesn't count). This should bring a few laughs and give you a glimpse of the individual personalities. Make a mental note of what you hear from each player. Some will be shy and quiet, others aggressive and outspoken; some will be humorous and full of bravado, others hesitant and self-conscious. This will give you your first insight into how to instruct each player. If a child is very shy, realize that this is the type of player who could easily be embarrassed by being singled out. Try to help the child along with a positive remark so as not to discourage future interactions.

Make a point of trying to talk to players individually before or after practice, or during water breaks, even if it's for just a few short seconds. You can learn a lot by looking each player in the eye and offering an encouraging word or making small talk about school, homework, or a new T-shirt. There's nothing like a pair of shocking-pink gym shoes to jump-start a get-to-know-you conversation.

During the first few practices, you also will begin to assess the differences in athletic ability and skill development. Some players will know something about the game, some will think they know something about the game, and others may be afraid to get involved. The first step toward helping each of these kids become basketball players is to notice how they're different and coach them accordingly.

You might see some huge differences in ability, especially early on. Don't write off kids just because they can't dribble without falling down; conversely, don't overrate the more graceful athletes. Know that the gap between the two extremes will narrow once you start teaching the kids the correct way to play the game. Gifted athletes may seem like the ones with the brightest futures, but kids who are good listeners, quick learners, and hard workers can catch up quickly.

Also, how a kid looks in practice is no indication of how that young athlete will play in a game. There are kids who look good in practice but crumble when someone starts keeping score. Conversely, the kid who seems uninspired by or indifferent to practice sometimes can really turn it on once the competitive juices get flowing. This is why it's important to always check the emotional temperature of the individuals on your team. The more you learn about the way their young minds tick, the better equipped you'll be to coach them.

Prepping for the First Game

If your team is scheduled to play its first game after only one or two practices, don't try to make everyone learn everything faster. This is called panicking. Teaching a crash course in basketball will only overwhelm the kids and jack up your blood pressure to catastrophic levels. You want to be on the sidelines with a clipboard, Coach, not in the hospital attached to an IV.

Remember, the only way you can get the results you want for your players is through time and repetition, neither of which you have right now. Dial down your expectations and begin laying the groundwork for your season with one fundamental at a time. Once you're done with introductions, include the following elements in the first couple of practices (the drills will be discussed in greater detail in chapters 3 and 4).

1. **Warm-ups and stretching.** Warm-ups are designed to increase core body temperature, increase blood flow to the muscles, increase range of motion, help mental preparation, and stretch muscles to prevent soreness. When children play, they rarely jump right into an activity, but naturally start slowly and build up to whatever game or fun thing they are doing. Similarly, a basketball warm-up is designed to gradually increase in tempo and intensity in preparation for the practice or game. Ideally, the warm-up should take 10 to 15 minutes and move directly into the day's basketball drills and activities, but adjust to an abbreviated version if you have less time.

   Figure 2.1 provides a basic but very functional warm-up routine. This will get everyone moving right away and prevent an outbreak of chitter-chatter among the restless players. The warm-up is built on dynamic stretching, which gently takes athletes to the limits of their range of motion. Dynamic stretching improves flexibility and helps prepare the players for an aerobic workout. Ideally, after the players have performed joint rotations, they should engage in at least five minutes of aerobic activity, such as jogging, jumping rope, or any other activity that will cause a similar increase in cardiovascular output (to get their blood pumping). If you have only 60 minutes for practice, you may need to reduce the number and duration of exercises so the warm-up does not cut significantly into the time for drills.

2. **Dribbling drills.** Ballhandling is difficult to master, but you may find one or two diamonds in the rough by observing how your young charges bounce a basketball. Can they dribble a ball the length of the floor without bouncing it off their toes? Can they control the ball with either hand?

3. **Passing drills.** Right away, you'll be able to assess the athleticism of the individual players by the way they throw and catch a ball. Some may be snapping chest passes and catching with soft hands. Others may have difficulty throwing the ball accurately even 10 feet or may back off and turn their head as they try to catch a pass.

4. **Free-throw shooting.** Here's another way to get a quick read of the team's relative skill level. Some kids may not even be able to reach the rim from the free-throw line. Encourage them to step closer. Others may be heaving the ball over the backboard because they have no clue how to shoot a basketball. One or two may be able to actually make a shot. File it all away for future reference, Coach. Right away, you'll have a sense of what each player needs to do to improve.

Figure 2.1   Sample Warm-Up Routine

Make sure the players breathe normally during these exercises and that they stretch their muscles only enough to feel mild tension, not pain. Each exercise should be done for approximately 20 yards at a walking pace, unless otherwise noted.

Toe and heel walk	Walk high on the toes, then only on the heels, and then alternate between toes and heels.
Knee hugs	Walk, pulling the knee up to the chest, take a step, and then hug the other knee.
Shin hugs or quad stretch	Gently pull the heel up to the butt (don't overstretch). Stretch the quadriceps and maintain balance. Athletes can place one hand on a wall to help maintain balance.
Lunges with a twist	Step forward with the right leg and almost touch the left knee to the floor. In the semi-kneeling position turn the upper body left, then right. Stand up and step with the other leg and repeat the twist to both sides.
Side lunges	Step to the side with a long lunge, keeping the upper body straight. Bring the legs together and repeat the lunge.
Straight-leg toe touches	While walking forward with the legs straight, bend forward to touch the toes. This hamstring stretch should be done slowly and gently, especially if the athletes are less flexible.
Leg kicks	Walk forward, kicking one leg and then the other. Kick gently at first and then higher as muscles loosen.
Side shuffle	Shuffle sideways, staying low and not crossing the legs. Increase speed and intensity as the exercise is mastered.
Carioca	Shuffle sideways by crossing one leg in front of the other and then crossing the same leg behind. Continue this pattern to stretch and increase flexibility in the hips. Repeat, going in the opposite direction with the other leg making the crossing steps.
High skips	Skip as high as possible, throwing the right hand in the air at the same time the right knee goes up, simulating a layup action. Repeat on the left side.
High knees	Run with a high knee lift and strong arm action.
Backward run	Alternately bring each heel to the butt and then step back as far as possible to run backward.
Straight-leg run	Run while keeping the legs straight, pulling them forward and then down. When done correctly, this exercise, which mimics a football player's celebratory run in the end zone, strengthens the muscles used in sprinting.

5. **Defensive slides.** Watching the players move from side to side and then drop-step backward down the floor while defending a ballhandler will give a coach a good idea of each player's footwork, quickness, and balance. (See chapter 4 for a detailed explanation of this skill.)

6. **Zone defensive set.** By setting up a zone defense (discussed in further detail in chapter 6), you will teach an essential building block of team defense: players shouldn't all run around and chase the ball. Along with defensive fundamentals, you start to lay the groundwork for basic defensive concepts. Players need to learn body position in relationship to their opponent and the basket they are defending.

   In a zone defense, an individual player's coverage area is greatly reduced compared to man-to-man defense. This is why it's best to start with a zone defense (while still keeping in mind that you will want your team to play mostly man-to-man defense by the time the season ends). But don't expect to nail all that down right away. In the first practice, you'll be doing well if you get the kids to understand the floor positioning of the 2-3 zone. Just keep building on the concepts bit by bit with each practice.

7. **Offensive scheme.** The pass-cut-replace offense (explained in chapter 5) is the easiest team offense to learn. It is especially useful because it involves all five players on the floor. It will take the players a few practices to fully understand it, but initially your mantra should be *pass and cut*. In other words, the players shouldn't stand around after getting rid of the ball. If you can get the players to cut toward the basket after making a pass, you'll be imparting a basic principle of any offense.

Figure 2.2 provides a sample practice plan incorporating all the necessary elements for an early-season practice. Each practice will be different, but the sample shows how a practice could be structured. It covers the basics and can help you quickly gauge your team's abilities in the areas of ballhandling, shooting, and defensive agility. Give the players at least one water break during a practice—more if the workout is longer than 60 minutes, is particularly stressful, or if conditions (such as heat or humidity) in the gym warrant it. This also gives you an opportunity to catch your breath, drink some water, and pop an aspirin or two as needed. Occasionally, the noise level in a small gym can be a little tough to take, even for the most seasoned coach.

You might also find that water breaks are a good time to set up any necessary equipment for the second half of practice or to make any adjustments in the practice schedule based on what's happened so far.

Figure 2.2 Sample Early-Season Practice Plan

Early in the season the coach should evaluate the players' individual abilities to get a handle on the relative strengths and weaknesses of the team. Practice time should be primarily devoted to individual skills to aid in this evaluation, while introducing a handful of basic team concepts.

Duration	Skill or activity	Exercises or drills by team experience level
5:00 to 5:02	Warm-up	Players jog around the court twice.
5:02 to 5:05	Stretching	Players stretch arms, shoulders, neck, back, and legs.
5:05 to 5:10	Dribbling	Starting from five lines of two at each baseline, with one ball per line, players do the following: Right-hand dribble down and back twice Left-hand dribble down and back twice Crossover, two dribbles right, two dribbles left, down and back twice
5:10 to 5:15	Passing	Pair up players with a ball. Have them stand 10 to 12 feet apart and practice chest passes, bounce passes, and overhead passes.
5:15 to 5:25	Free-throw shooting	Divide the players up equally at each available basket and have them rotate around the free-throw lanes, shooting two free throws at a time for a maximum of 10 each. The non-shooting players should rebound and return the ball quickly to the shooter. Have the non-shooting players clap once for a miss, twice for a make to keep them involved.
Water break		
5:30 to 5:40	Defensive drill	Z Slides (page 89): Establish proper defensive stance, then work on defensive footwork. Defenders slide side to side and work to stay in front of the dribbler the length of the court.
5:40 to 5:50	Offensive scheme	Pass-cut-replace
5:50 to 6:00	Defensive set	2-3 zone

Breaks can also be a good time to talk to a player or two individually to offer either encouragement (*Your free throws are looking really good today. Have you been working on them at home?*) or advice (*Your dribbling is getting better all the time—if you keep working on your left hand, you're going to be a very good ballhandler*).

Sizing Up Your Team

In the first practices, you'll have to make some decisions about how you want to use your players in the first game. How do you decide who plays where? You have a dozen kids in the gym, and the obvious decision is to divide the team according to height: the tallest kids are your centers and forwards, the smaller ones your guards. But height isn't always the best indicator of what position a player is suited for.

Young athletes will grow at different rates. Skills and comprehension will develop at different times. Some kids may be accomplished dribblers; others may think that dribbling is something you do with your feet and a soccer ball. You will have to adjust your expectations for each of these different levels accordingly. Learning and playing all the different positions will help these young players understand through experience what it takes to do each job on the court.

Sometimes tall players develop into terrific point guards, and smaller kids become relentless rebounders and end up becoming power forwards. It's impossible to tell. That's why it's so important to rotate novice basketball players through all the positions in practice and games to give them a taste of every responsibility on the court and also to give you, the coach, a handle on their individual strengths and weaknesses. It also will challenge each player to stay focused and learn something new, and you will keep the interest of all your players. For some players, learning even one position will be a hurdle that may require all season to overcome. Others will quickly adapt to anything you throw at them. Again, adjust and improvise as you go.

By the end of your first season, you'll have a feel for where a kid belongs on the basketball court. But early on, encourage the players to move out of their expected positions before they become comfort zones. Give the tall, gangly kid a shot at point guard. Let the short, stocky player have an opportunity to throw a few moves in the low post. The key is not to lock a kid into a position too soon but to unlock the hidden player within. Tell your players that the more positions they learn, the more valuable they will be to their team and their teammates.

Creating Successful Practice Plans

After you've survived the initial practices and have come to know your players better and understand their strengths and weaknesses, you'll need to design practices that make the most of your team's allotted gym time. One of the biggest challenges for a coach is to plan practices that will keep the athletes eager and engaged from start to finish. When's the time to switch drills? When does just enough become too much? You'll know by the distracted looks on the kids' faces and the increased level of chitchat about important nonbasketball matters such as instant messaging.

The last thing you want is a bunch of kids sleepwalking through the drills because they're bored. No two practices will be exactly alike, and the emphasis of the practices should constantly evolve as the season progresses, but the fundamentals that you cover will be the same throughout the season. You'll use some drills at nearly every practice, especially early in the season, but vary the rest. Many of the remaining chapters in this book provide basic drills to teach key fundamentals. Along the way, you will find certain drills that the kids like best, and you can save these to reward them for a job well done or to give them a break.

Here are the key areas to focus on for each practice throughout the season.

1. **Warm-ups and stretching.** Even young muscles need to be stretched before every workout. The toughest part of every practice will be getting started; getting the players on the floor to stretch can use up 5 to 10 minutes, which is a huge percentage of your 60 minutes. So get going on time, even if kids are still straggling into the gym. Let them join the warm-ups in progress, and send the not-so-subtle message that it's important to show up on time.

2. **Ballhandling.** In many ways, this is the key to your team's success and your players' development. It should be part of nearly every practice. Chapter 3 provides a variety of drills to choose from.

3. **Shooting.** Players need to learn to shoot everything from layups to free throws with proper technique, but doing so is an ongoing process. You'll find more on this in chapter 3.

4. **Individual defensive skill fundamentals and defensive sets.** Here's where you start implementing team concepts. See chapters 4 and 6 for details.

5. **Individual offensive skill fundamentals and the pass-cut-replace offense.** And here's how your team learns to work together to produce points. See chapters 3 and 5 for specific information.

This is a short list, and it doesn't cover all the ground necessary to shape a team. But it's a place to start, especially with limited practice time. In the first practice, focus on individual skills on offense and defense, but by the second practice, start addressing the team concepts. You'll want to get these in place as early as possible and then refine both the team concepts and the individual skills as the season goes along. Start familiarizing your team with zone defense, man-to-man defense, and the pass-cut-replace offense as soon as possible so you have something to work with during the games. Individual skills and fundamentals should be part of at least every other practice through the end of the season. They not only provide a foundation for defensive and offensive team concepts and make them easier for the kids to understand, but they also help the kids execute those team concepts with greater efficiency.

Figure 2.3 provides a sample plan for a typical 60-minute midseason practice. By this time, the players should have at least a basic knowledge of individual fundamentals and can begin focusing on broader team concepts. By the time you finish this book, you will be able to move a number of drills in and out of this basic template with the goal of working on individual offensive and defensive skills as well as team concepts in each practice. Sixty minutes is not a lot of time, but a well-designed practice should allow a team to run through four or five drills.

To pull this off, you'll need to stick to a schedule and watch the clock. Wear a watch (or carry a cell phone) so you don't lose track. It's amazing how quickly the minutes can fly when you're introducing a new skill and the players are buzzing with excitement and confusion. Before you know it, practice is nearly over and you've managed to run only one or two things. So don't linger too long in any one area, but don't rush just to stay on schedule. Know that you will return to each of these areas at later practices; there's no need to cram. Alternate the speed and skill sets required for each section of practice. Don't do similar things back to back, such as working on a defensive set, then an offensive play, where movement is minimal and more explaining needs to be done. Mix in a fast-moving drill to shake up the tempo and burn off some restless energy.

During individual drills, every player will be involved. During team drills, don't use the same five players all the time to demonstrate points. Alternate the players and let everyone have a chance. This reinforces the notion that every player is critical to the team's success. Keep the kids on the sidelines involved by asking them questions as you work on the floor with some of their teammates (*Jenny, where do you think Molly should be on this play?*).

Sometimes, you will need to take more time to explain an area of special importance if the kids aren't too far along as basketball players. No need

Figure 2.3   Sample Midseason Practice Plan

By this point in the season, no two practices should be exactly alike. Try to balance each session with individual defensive and offensive drills. Introduce defensive sets and offensive plays that can be used in games. Consult the appropriate chapter for information on each drill.

Duration	Skill or activity	Exercises or drills by team experience level
5:00 to 5:02	Warm-up	Players jog around the court twice.
5:02 to 5:05	Stretching	Players stretch arms, shoulders, neck, back, legs.
5:05 to 5:10	Offensive drill	Give-and-go (page 70): This drill emphasizes ball movement, footwork, shooting, and cutting to the basket; it's also a great way to get the kids moving early in the practice.
5:10 to 5:15	Dribbling	Hand speed stationary dribbling (page 58): Use one ball per player, or one ball shared by two players, at center court.
5:15 to 5:25	Defensive drill	Shell (page 98): This drill emphasizes man-to-man concepts of jumping to the ball, moving to the help line, closing out, putting a hand in the passing lane, and staying open to the ball.
Water break		
5:30 to 5:40	Offensive scheme	Four-out, one-in offense (page 116)
5:40 to 6:00	Special plays	Out of bounds plays: Stack, hawk, and sideline (pages 140, 141, and 142)

to fret; you can always pick up where you left off at the next practice. You may also encounter situations in which some members of your team have locked onto a new skill while others are struggling. Young players rarely learn at the same pace. The better athletes may seem to thrive from the start, so what do you do about the less gifted ones? How can you help them keep pace and feel like a part of the team?

If you aren't working with assistant coaches, ask the players who need more help to come to practice a little early or stay a bit later after practice. Go over one area of the game you would like them to improve and give them a drill to work on at home. Point out to the player that his eagerness to learn is a great start to becoming a good basketball player. For every point you make about improving a player's game, give two compliments: *I really like the way you hustle in these drills, and your shot is looking better all the time. Now let's work on your dribbling a little bit.* If the player can't work on something at home, for whatever reason, assure the player that if he keeps coming to practice and working hard, good things will happen. He'll get it eventually, and there's no need to worry. Your team has a whole season to improve.

If you do have assistants, allocate individual time for the less-gifted players during practice while the rest of the team is running through drills. Don't have them stray from the main group for too long, but a little one-on-one attention can go a long way in building a new player's game and confidence.

At the end of each practice, tell your players what you'd like them to work on at home and give them some insight about what the team will be working on next. It can be helpful to say things such as, *We're getting better at ballhandling, but it's not enough to just practice once or twice a week. You need to go home and work on these things on your own for 15 minutes a day. If you do, you're going to be terrific ballhandlers in a few months and we're going to have a lot of fun playing the games.*

If you have 90 minutes allotted for practice, you can start to introduce team concepts on offense and defense sooner in the season. As the season progresses, you can alternate individual skill work with team-concept drills on offense and defense. Use the games as a springboard for what needs to be addressed in subsequent practices. If the team is playing well offensively during games, but allowing too many easy layups on defense, spend more time at the next practice working on defensive skills and team defense.

Remember to allow about 10 to 15 minutes per drill; it's difficult to accomplish much in a shorter period of time, and anything longer will test the kids' (and inevitably the coach's) patience. The longer the practice, the more critical it is for the coach to keep an eye on pacing. Be sure to alternate strenuous drills with slower, more cerebral ones so the kids don't get restless. The best way to get the kids' attention is to run them hard in one drill, then hit them with verbal information in a new, slower-paced drill while they're catching their breath.

Again, don't spend too much time in any one area. Once the kids tune out of a drill, they start going through the motions and they stop learning. A coach needs to recognize this and be prepared to move the kids into a new drill before they drift off to never-never land. Once they go there, it's tough to get them back. So reel them in before they drift with a change of pace and a new challenge. Then, at the next practice, return to the drill you abandoned when you have their attention again.

After practice, evaluate in private where players are progressing fastest and slowest and make notes if necessary to remind yourself. Repetition will be the key to learning what you have taught. Now set up your next practice session. Juggle new drills with older ones, making sure to touch on each fundamental (passing, dribbling, shooting, offense, and defense). As the season progresses, you will find that you have to explain less, because the players will become familiar with the different drills and jump into them more rapidly. Encourage the kids who know how to do a particular drill to take the lead and remind the others how it's done. As their confidence grows, your hair should stop falling out.

Shaping Your Team Over a Season

It's best to lay the groundwork for team concepts of offense and defense from the first practice. It takes time to learn how to run an offense and play proper team defense, but it's never too early to start asking players to think as a team. From the first game, you should encourage the players to execute basic team fundamentals on offense (pass, cut, and replace) and defense (cover a zone instead of a man, and don't cluster to the ball). As the season moves on, they will learn more sophisticated defensive and offensive sets.

If you have the practice time before your first game, focus on the defensive and offensive skills and drills outlined in chapters 3 and 4. These concepts are the foundation on which you must build your team.

Introduction of defensive and offensive sets should be built a step at a time. Defensive schemes are built from one player up to five. To teach team defense you start with individual skills, then move to two players and how they need to work together, then three players, and so on. Offensive sets are no different. The offense should be introduced in parts, until the players grasp each one. You will not be able to teach an offense or defense in one practice. Again, think long term: You're building a youth basketball team over a season, not creating an instant NBA title contender.

Basketball has five positions that demand certain skills sets, some of which overlap. Typically, positions 1 and 2 are guard positions, in which ballhandling and outside shooting are at a premium. Position 3 is a small forward, which combines the skills of a guard with some of the rebounding demanded of taller players. Positions 4 and 5 are forward-center positions, which emphasize rebounding, inside shooting, and interior defense. Keep these numbers in mind; they will be used throughout the book to identify individual players in offensive schemes and defensive sets.

As noted earlier, it's not a good idea to lock down a young player to one position. As the season progresses, give each player a chance to play every position. Over time, a player's affinity for a certain position might become obvious. But it's best in practices to keep the players rotating through all the positions so they can learn everyone's responsibility on the court.

Equal playing time is a must. Eventually, you will hit on combinations of players that work well together, but it's best to keep mixing and mingling so that the weaker players aren't all on the court at the same time. Eventually, you may find mixes of stronger and weaker players that work well together. Encourage that sort of familiarity, and give these players a chance to further develop their chemistry in games and in practice.

Emphasizing Fun

To keep practices from getting too rigid and serious, keep things upbeat. You don't want a gigglefest breaking out every other minute, but underlying every drill is the idea that basketball should be fun. And working hard can make the game even more fun. When players learn a skill, there is a sense of accomplishment that is its own reward. But young players can't be expected to keep their eyes on the prize all the time. They can be pushed to improve, but only so much and so far.

A coach can't keep her pedal to the metal throughout a 60- or 90-minute practice and expect a dozen six-year-olds to continually respond. It's OK to introduce a few drills just for kicks, to spice up a season and let the kids have a few laughs before going back to skill training. As a bonus, the giggle games that follow do emphasize several teaching points; they just do it in a way that doesn't seem all that serious.

Drill 1 Knockout

EQUIPMENT   Two basketballs

PURPOSE   This activity helps sharpen players' shooting.

PROCEDURE   Create one line at the free-throw line (the line can be moved closer to the basket for younger players). If enough baskets are available, create lines of no more than 10 players each. The first two players should each have a basketball. The game starts when player 1 shoots a free throw. If the shot is made, player 1 goes to the end of the line, and player 2 shoots a free throw. If player 1 misses the free throw, he must retrieve the basketball and make a layup before player 2 makes a free-throw or layup. If player 2 makes a shot before player 1, player 1 is knocked out of the game. The rest of the players in line follow the same procedure, and the pattern continues until one player is left.

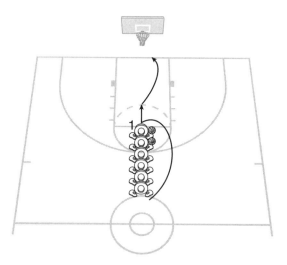

Drill 2 Two-Player Passing

🏀 BEGINNER

EQUIPMENT   One ball for every two players

PURPOSE   This will help players develop accuracy when passing to a moving target.

PROCEDURE   Start with two lines about 10 feet apart at the baseline, with one line near the sideline and one near the nearest free-throw lane line. The distance between the two lines can vary depending on age, strength, and ability of the players. Start out with a small distance between the players and increase as they begin to understand the drill. Players should stay on their half of the court and run toward the opposite baseline passing the ball back and forth to each other. Once players reach the opposite baseline, they move to the other half of the court. The player running nearest the sideline should sprint to the opposite side-

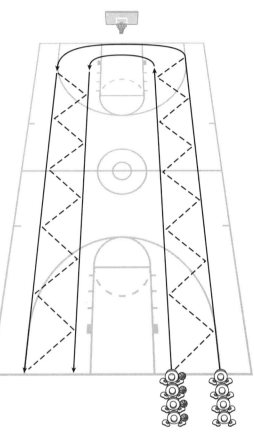

line and the player in the middle moves to the other free-throw lane line. The drill continues as the two players run down the opposite half of the court back to the original baseline.

COACHING POINTS   Focus on running straight ahead. Players should have feet, hips, and shoulders facing the basket as much as possible while performing the drill. Teammates should lead each other with the pass.

Drill 3 Three-Man Weave

⊕⊕ INTERMEDIATE

EQUIPMENT   One ball for three players

PURPOSE   Players learn to pass to a moving teammate and fill lanes for a fast break

PROCEDURE   Form three lines at the baseline: one in the middle and one on each side of the middle line. Adjust the distance between the middle line and the lines on the sides based on the relative age of the players and their ability to pass the basketball at a distance. When in doubt, start the lines closer together, and then spread them out as the players' understanding of the drill and passing ability improve.

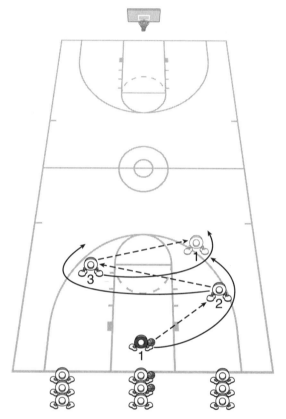

Player 1 in the center line starts with the basketball. A pass is made to player 2 (the first player in either of the lines on the side). Player 1 then runs and weaves behind player 2 while player 2 passes to player 3 (the first player in the line on the opposite side) and runs or weaves behind player 3. Player 3 then passes to player 1 and runs and weaves behind player 1, and so on. The three continue down the floor until they reach the opposite baseline. The drill can end with a scoring attempt at the opposite end of the floor by a player who receives a pass close enough to attempt a layup without needing to dribble.

COACHING POINTS   The passer weaves down the floor by moving behind the pass receiver. Passes should lead the receiver, and the three players should move the ball rapidly down the floor without dribbling. Emphasize that for the drill to succeed, players must move in lanes down the floor and must run continuously during the drill. They should not stop or stand to wait for a pass. This will be important when teaching your players how to run a fast break.

The Coach's Clipboard

✔ Keep the show moving; don't spend too much time on one drill.

✔ Get to the point. Save the speeches.

✔ Teach by asking questions.

✔ Take charge with a plan from the first minute.

✔ Guide, don't demand.

✔ When in doubt, use humor.

✔ Strive for improvement, not perfection.

✔ Keep it simple, especially in the first few practices.

✔ Don't rush to judge your players; talent doesn't always reveal itself right away.

✔ Design practices to keep all the players involved as much as possible.

✔ It's not only OK to have fun, it's encouraged!

Developing Offensive Skills With 10 Simple Drills

Who doesn't like to score? It's not as easy as it looks, obviously, but it sure can be fun to learn. So let's focus on the offensive side of basketball first. In this chapter, we'll pinpoint drills to help your players learn the skills they'll need to run an offense and ultimately light up the opposing team for 10 to 12 points a game. Yes, go ahead and laugh: 10 to 12 points? Lower your expectations, Coach. If you can get your group to score in double figures the first time out, that's an accomplishment.

Do not expect your team to turn into an offensive juggernaut right away. It's one thing to shoot layups in the driveway or gym, but quite another to find a path to the basket against five jumpy defenders in the heat of a game. So do yourself a favor and don't keep track of your team's shooting percentage for the first few games. It's bad for your health and for your team's self-esteem.

You might find yourself depressed as you stare at field-goal statistics such as 2-for-21, 3-for-27, and so on. Yes, it can get that bad, and sometimes worse. It's not that unusual for a really inexperienced team to be shut out for a half or even an entire game when up against a slightly bigger, faster, more skilled opponent. Do not be discouraged. At first, expect the worst when it comes to quality offensive basketball. Celebrate every basket is if it were a lunar eclipse: a rare and wondrous event.

But know that improvement can be swift if you tweak your mindset just a bit. Better to measure your team's growth by the number of shots they take in each game. In those dire statistics just cited, the fact that the team managed to launch 21 shots in a game is worth noting. It's a way to turn a negative (*Wow, we sure couldn't score today*) into a positive (*Wow, we managed to work close enough to the hoop to get a ton of shots*). It's a huge accomplishment for a young team to work the basketball close enough to actually take a shot that clanks off the rim or backboard. If your team can get shots, then it can eventually score baskets.

As the team progresses, refine that formula for success a bit: Start adding up quality shots, rather than the prayers that have no chance of going in. One of the key points of this chapter is teaching your players proper shooting technique so they know in practice what a quality shot feels like. Once they start getting those kinds of shots in games, they're on their way to scoring more points, and the 10 drills in this chapter will point your group of eager scoring machines in the right direction.

Learning the fundamentals is crucial, but the process of mastering them can be somewhat tiresome because it requires repetition and patience—skills that squirmy youngsters don't normally possess. So it's important to focus on keeping things fun and varied and never lingering too long in one area. It's best to build up offensive skills in increments over a long period, rather than force-feeding them to your players in extended sessions. It's also important to keep the drills age appropriate; each drill can be tailored to the strength, size, and maturity of your players.

Great basketball players are built from the ground up. You may shoot and dribble with your hands, but it all starts with proper footwork. The motto of every great basketball team can be boiled down to the title of an old Little Feat song: "Feats don't fail me now!" or in this case, "*Feets* don't fail me now!" So let's get to work on making the feet perform at a championship level.

Passing and Catching

Passing and catching seem so basic that they're easily overlooked. Don't make that mistake, Coach. Otherwise, you'll watch the turnovers pile up and the hair fall in clumps from your aching head. These two vital skills should be worked on at every practice.

At younger age levels, players don't yet have the muscle to execute long passes or the skills to consistently receive a pass. But teaching simple passing and receiving techniques will go a long way toward building the players' confidence in themselves and one another. It's amazing how quickly a group of players can evolve into a team when they realize that when they throw a pass to another player, it will be caught instead of fumbled into a turnover. The foundation for that trust can be built from your first practice.

You'll need to teach your team how to properly perform chest, bounce, and overhead passes. In game situations, each of these passes will play an important role, which is why it's essential to work on them in practice. Consider how many passes are attempted in each game. Then consider how many are thrown out of bounds, off a receiver's shoe tops or knees, over everybody's heads, or into an opponent's hands. It doesn't matter how many great shooters or defenders you have—if your team can't pass and catch, it can't win. In addition, lots of drills in practice depend on being able to pass and catch. A bad pass means the drill breaks down, and a lot of time and energy are wasted chasing errant throws.

Just as important is the pass that doesn't merely reach its target but that leads directly to a score. The location of the setup pass can be the difference between a field goal and a miss. Hit a teammate in her outstretched hands as she cuts to the basket, and the timing and the chances of making the shot are enhanced. Fling the pass just slightly behind the cutter, and the timing is thrown off and the chances of an errant shot soar.

So it's important to cover the passing-and-catching basics from the first practice and continue to build on them. Players need to learn how to hit a stationary target (the player with outstretched hands), then develop a sense of how to hit a moving target (the player cutting to the basket). Through these drills, passers learn how to throw the ball to a spot where the receiver will be. This will take some practice, but it's a skill that can be introduced, practiced, and refined quickly over the course of a few weeks.

Chest Pass   The chest pass is the most common pass in basketball and will be used most frequently in games. To teach the chest pass, have the passer hold a ball at chest level with both hands, knees slightly bent, and feet shoulder-width apart (see figure 3.1a). The passer should then square up to the target with both shoulders, establish a pivot foot and then step with the opposite foot, and pass the ball to the partner, finishing with hands fully extended and thumbs pointing in and down (see figure 3.1b). The passer should focus on stepping into the pass and on snapping the pass with both hands so that the basketball travels into the hands of the receiver at about chest level. Tell players to *make it zing.*

Even at an early age, it's important to emphasize that the ball should stay in flight for as little time as possible. The longer it takes for the pass to reach the receiver, the easier it is for the opposing team to intercept the ball. So, discourage high-arching moon-balls and the soft one-handed toss. Make it clear that a great pass isn't just the product of a strong arm. A player who relies on just his arm to make a pass will be throwing the ball away more often than not. But even the smallest, scrawniest player on the court can deliver a smart pass by using his entire body.

Figure 3.1   Proper technique for executing a chest pass.

Bounce Pass   The bounce pass is especially useful for smaller players in game situations. Rather than throw a pass around or over the long arms of taller players, the smaller player can use a bounce pass to reach the target. It's much easier to throw a pass underneath those big trees clogging the lane than to throw over them.

The starting position for the bounce pass is to hold the ball at chest level with both hands. Knees should be slightly bent and feet should be shoulder-width apart (see figure 3.2*a*). To complete the pass, the passer should step with the lead foot, or non-pivot foot, and pass the ball to a partner with a popping action or snap, finishing with hands out, thumbs pointing in and down (see figure 3.2*b*). The basketball should hit the floor about two-thirds to three-quarters of the distance from the passer. The ball should arrive at the midsection or waist of the teammate.

Again, speed counts. The bounce pass should skip into the receiver's hands. Many passers tend to start the bounce too high, at their chin, and let the ball drop to the floor. Like the chest pass, the bounce pass should have some zing to it: It should hit the floor and pop into the receiver's hands. Remind your players to make it pop, not plop.

Figure 3.2   Proper technique for executing a bounce pass.

Overhead Pass   The overhead pass is useful in game situations for tall players who can get the ball to a teammate by passing over the outstretched arms of smaller defensive players. It is also the ideal pass for starting a fast break after a defensive rebound because it enables rebounders to keep the ball high (and more difficult for the defense to tie up) as they pivot away from the basket and look to pass.

The starting position for the overhead pass is to hold the ball just overhead with both hands (see figure 3.3*a*). Knees should be slightly bent and feet should be shoulder-width apart. The player should then step with the lead foot, or non-pivot foot, and with both hands throw the ball to a partner (see figure 3.3*b*).

This is a tough pass to master, especially for younger players who may not be strong enough yet to throw the ball overhead. Only the strongest players will be able to put the proper amount of snap on the ball to reach the target. But it is still a good pass for every player to work on in practice because it doubles as a strengthening exercise for the arms, shoulders, and upper back. Bigger players will love this pass because they can use it to keep the ball high after a rebound and deliver a quick pass (an outlet pass) to a guard racing up the court for a layup.

Figure 3.3   Proper technique for executing an overhead pass.

Catching a Pass   Throwing the pass is only half the job. Catching the pass makes the passer look great. There is only one small catch (so to speak): Not every pass will be perfect. It's important for the passer and receiver to have confidence in each other, and building that trust starts in practice. To catch a pass, players should get ready with both feet down, knees slightly bent, hands out, elbows slightly flexed (see figure 3.4a). Pass receivers should extend their hands, providing a target for the passer. They should then step toward the passer and meet the ball (see figure 3.4b).

If the receiver is passive, a defender can easily step in front of the pass and intercept it. The passer often gets the blame, but the wait-and-see receiver is equally at fault. It's important for receivers to recognize their responsibility in completing a pass, and the coach needs to watch for this in practice and in games. Both passer and receiver have a role in cutting down the amount of time a pass is in the air; the longer it's airborne, the easier it is to intercept. They need to work together as teammates. Passers need to make a sharp pass. Receivers should never wait for the ball to arrive. They need to be a little impatient and meet it a step sooner. They should always be thinking *step to the ball*.

At first, some smaller players may have difficulty even catching a pass. Lack of focus may be a problem, but the coach can correct it by reminding players to keep their eyes on the ball. This simple but

Figure 3.4 To catch a pass, players should be in a receiving position and then meet the ball.

timeless piece of advice usually eliminates most pass-catching problems. Receivers need to watch the ball and guide it into their hands with their eyes. They should catch the ball with their hands without cradling it to the chest or tummy. Try to give the ball a soft landing by cushioning the ball just as it meets the skin.

Smaller and younger players may also have a fear of catching a relatively large thrown object. It can be intimidating. So it's best not to start by having them catch passes from bigger, stronger teammates who can quickly turn a game of catch into dodgeball by bouncing balls off the knees and forehead of a novice pass-catcher. Start them off by catching softer passes and gradually develop their confidence over time. Pair them with players of similar stature and have them work together on progressing as passers and catchers.

Dribbling

Just about anyone can bounce a basketball a few times. But while under pressure in a game, most young players struggle to keep the ball from bouncing off their shoes or hitting them in the nose. You're lucky to find one or two decent ballhandlers on any youth basketball team. One of the reasons so few kids can handle the ball is that not enough time is devoted to ballhandling in practice. Like passing or catching a basketball, dribbling is one of the game's fundamentals that must be developed carefully.

New coaches tend to focus on running plays and scoring baskets, while overlooking the fundamentals that make or break a team. Without ballhandlers, a team may not even get a shot at the basket, let alone score a point in a game. Getting the ball past half-court without committing a turnover and then actually working the ball close enough to launch a shot at the basket can be a huge accomplishment for a young team and should be celebrated. (Handstands are optional.) You'll need good ballhandlers to get there.

Dribbling is the ability to bounce a basketball under control. The longer the ball is out of a dribbler's hands, the better chance for the dribbler to lose control of the ball. To maintain control of the dribble, players must keep their arm and elbow free (avoid locking the elbow to the hip), and keep the dribble below waist level. The hand, including the fingertips, should push the basketball firmly to the floor.

The best players can dribble a basketball with either hand. The ball appears as if it's an extension of the hand, and the player never once has to look at the ball while moving it from side to side, front to back, through the legs, and around the back. Unfortunately, players of this caliber are usually found on the Harlem Globetrotters, not on youth basketball teams. Such players rarely just drop into a team's lap. They're made during hours of practice. And those hours will be filled with lots of stumbling, bumbling, and fumbling.

More likely, a coach will be confronted with a dozen kids who may or may not be able to dribble in a straight line with their dominant hand (usually, their right hand), much less with their nondominant hand. Do not fret. Do not panic. Do not expect Magic Johnson to emerge from your squirming mother lode of talent after one practice. Start with the basics.

First on the list is to get the kids to avoid slapping the ball. This is not dribbling. This is not ballhandling. This is basketball abuse. Instead, encourage the players to handle the ball with the "pads" on their hands; these can be found at the fingertips and the top of the palm. The ball should feel like it's nestling in the hand and fingers for a split second before it returns to the ground, as if it were on an invisible yo-yo string. The principle here is the same as in catching a pass; players should feel like they are briefly "catching" the ball as it rises from the floor. The hand meets the ball and then cushions it for a split second, then firmly snaps it back to the floor with a flick of the fingers and a snap of the wrist.

Body position is important. Players inevitably like to stand tall when they're first dribbling a ball, and this erect posture requires the ball to travel a greater distance between the floor and the hand. Minimize that distance. Encourage players to shorten the distance between hand and floor by bending the knees slightly when they dribble and dropping the rear end a bit (see figure 3.5). The ball should never rise above the waist or hips, and if the knees are bent, that should keep the ball no more than two feet above the ground at any time. This makes the ball a lot tougher for the defense to steal and a lot easier for the ballhandler to control.

Figure 3.5 Proper body position for dribbling.

For your shorter players, point out what a huge advantage they have when it comes to handling the ball. If they work on keeping the ball low and controlling it, they can break down almost any defense. For your taller players, focus them on bending their knees and emphasizing a low, controlled dribble to make the ball a less inviting target. If they stand fully erect while dribbling, they will invite steals and turnovers.

Teach players to keep the head up, eyes focused on the floor ahead. The person handling the ball needs to see where the defense is, and where her teammates are. Players' eyes will naturally gravitate toward the ball as they learn how to dribble, but they need to be reminded early and often that looking at the ball will not help them dribble better. In fact, it will lead to even more turnovers because they won't see where they're going. Remind them that when they ride their bikes they don't look at the pedals; they look at the road ahead so they don't crash. The same "rules of the road" apply to dribbling a basketball.

Dribbling with either hand is important but extremely difficult to master. In youth basketball, it's not uncommon to see players dribbling with their strong hand more than 90 percent of the time. Players who lack confidence in the nondominant hand become much more predictable and easier to defend. So it's imperative that dribbling drills emphasize that players learn how to handle the ball with both hands and master the crossover, in which the ball is transferred from one hand to the other while the player is moving up the floor. On the crossover dribble, players must keep the ball low (below the knees) and the receiving hand low and ready to receive the ball as it is transferred from the opposite hand. When a right-handed player drives to his left in a game using the left hand, it should warrant a shout of encouragement from the coach and high fives for the player when he returns to the bench. These are the kind of measuring sticks a coach should use to gauge the players' improvement, not wins and losses.

There are thousands of dribbling drills to choose from. How do you know which ones will work for you and your team? Start by thinking of the drills in two forms: stationary ballhandling and dribbling. Both types are presented in this chapter. With this approach players learn that before they can dribble a ball expertly they must learn how to handle it. It's important to build the handling part before you begin to actually move with the ball. Building handles (see hand speed stationary dribbling on page 58) is the skill of using your hands to control the ball. Developing hand speed lays the groundwork for dribbling.

Shooting

Now the fun starts. Everybody likes to score, but very few people know how to shoot. In youth basketball, players are so consumed with reaching the rim that they don't care how they do it. They'll throw the ball any which way to get it near the hoop. This can make for some creative on-the-fly decision making as players try to score by any means necessary: over the shoulder, behind the head, backing up, falling down, through the legs. In a kid's world, it's all about whatever it takes, right?

So the first question a coach needs her little scoring machines to understand and answer is, *What is a good shot?* In youth basketball, a few factors constitute a good shot. Is the shooter open? That is, is the shooter a safe distance from the opponent so the ball won't be blocked? Is the shot within shooting range—can the shooter easily reach the basket using proper technique? And is the shot the best opportunity to score, or is there a teammate closer to the basket who would have an even better scoring opportunity?

Each outside shot uses basically the same technique. Shoulders should be relaxed and squared up to the rim, with the feet evenly spaced and shoulder-width apart (see figure 3.6). The shooting hand should grip the ball with the pads (fingertips and top of the palm) on the seams, slightly to the right of center if the right hand is being used and slightly to the left of center if the left hand is used. The guide (nondominant) hand should lightly grip the ball on the outside edge of the ball opposite the shooting (dominant) hand.

Figure 3.6 Proper shot pocket position.

Each shot should begin with the ball in the shot pocket, about waist high, at a relaxed distance from the body with elbows bent. Location of the elbow as the ball is placed in the shot pocket is key. If the shooting elbow is out too far ahead of the body, the ball will be too far away from the shot pocket. If the elbow is too far behind the body, the ball will be jammed into the player's gut. The ideal position for the shooting elbow is next to or alongside the body. Knees should also be slightly bent, and the head should be level.

The shooter then lifts the ball to the face until the elbow and upper arm of the shooting arm are parallel or almost parallel to the floor. As the ball is lifted, the knees bend farther. This is called a *coil* and helps give the shot proper rhythm (see figure 3.7).

The ball should move in one continuous smooth motion through the area in front of the face and as the shooting arm extends above the head as the ball is being released. The head should remain level through the entire motion. The shooter should push up onto the toes and finish with the shooting arm extended above the head with the wrist snapping the ball at the finish. The middle and index fingers should point directly at the rim (see figure 3.8).

Figure 3.7 Proper coil technique.

Figure 3.8 Proper release of the ball.

Players can work on this technique by taking a series of shots a few feet from the basket. A lot of kids like to mess around by taking impossible shots from midcourt and beyond as they wait for practice to begin. These shots are fun to try in playground games like H-O-R-S-E, but they don't produce great shooters. Players who work on their shooting form by taking 20 to 25 shots a day (or more) a few feet away from the rim at the gym or in their driveway will build muscle memory and rock-solid technique that will lead to more baskets in games.

Layups

The outcome of most basketball games turns on the execution—or the lack of execution—of a few fundamentals. In most games, on up to the professional level, whichever team scores the most layups and prevents the most layups usually wins. *Layups! If we'd only made our layups!* If you've ever talked to a coach after a losing game, you're likely to hear that lament a few thousand times. Yes, missed layups can drive any coach nuts. And, yes, most missed layups can be traced to lousy technique. The way out of the loony bin starts on the first day of practice with players learning the proper technique.

Layups are the cornerstone shot of any offense. But they are not an easy skill to learn. Many high school players don't have the proper footwork to make a layup, can't make one with either hand, or sabotage a good shot by taking a bad route to the basket. For the grade-school beginner to master this skill, it should be broken down into parts. Once again, feet first!

Many layups succeed or fail based on the path the shooter takes to the basket. The best angle for a layup is through "the gate," the point between the low block and first small hash mark on the free-throw lane line. It's amazing how much better shooting percentage will get once players start paying attention to this often overlooked detail. Instead of finding themselves too far under the basket to use the backboard properly or too far away so that they end up taking a running jump shot, the through-the-gate route gives the shooter an inviting 45-degree angle to the backboard, ideal for banking the ball into the basket.

Footwork is important. Coaches should have the players start several steps away from the basket and choreograph their footwork on how to approach the basket. For right-hand layups, players step with their left foot (see figure 3.9*a*) and go up with their right leg and right arm. They should cradle the ball slightly to the left of their bodies and bring the ball through the area in front of their face before finishing with the right hand in an open position toward the basket (see figure 3.9*b*). Left-hand layups are just the opposite. Players step with the right foot and go up with the left leg and left arm. Players cradle the ball slightly to the right of their bodies and bring the ball through the area in front of their face before finishing with the left hand open to the basket.

For beginning players, work on the footwork without a basketball at first, then add the ball without requiring a dribble. Once the footwork and shot technique have been grasped, add the dribble. Most backboards have a painted square above the rim. Players need to see the square and aim for the inside of the square when they shoot a layup. So encourage players to have their head level and eyes up as they approach the rim. Keep in mind that at younger ages, traveling viola-

Figure 3.9 Proper footwork and shot technique for a right-hand layup.

tions might not be called during games as much, and in some cases not at all. Shooting a layup could take several practices to learn, and some players may require even more time. Once the players have the proper footwork down and can combine it with dribbling, two more ingredients are required:

- **Speed.** Players need to accelerate toward the basket as they prepare to shoot a layup. The faster a player is able to approach the basket, the better able the player is to launch off the floor and toward the rim with the ball.
- **Ball position.** As players step through the gate toward the rim, they should use the cradle technique to slow down slightly so that they can move the ball across their bodies into the launch position, up through the face area to the basket for a soft finish.

Players should work on mastering the footwork from both sides of the basket. Launching off the proper foot on either side of the basket is crucial to making the layup. Encourage the players to use the left hand and right hand from the appropriate side of the basket, even if they continuously miss the shot with their weaker hand. Applaud the effort, regardless of the results. At this stage, getting a player to use either hand for dribbling and shooting layups is a huge accomplishment and should be acknowledged.

Developing a reward system for making a layup or dribbling in for a basket with the off hand is left up to the discretion and budget of the individual coach. Some coaches would call these bribes, and others would call them inducements. But occasionally, they are a great way to get the attention of players who essentially try to play the game with one hand tied behind their back.

Movement and Footwork

Movement and footwork skills continue our "*Feets* Don't Fail Me Now" saga. Once players have begun learning the basics of ballhandling and shooting, these skills will prove vital during games and should be worked on in practice as a way to keep the ball moving on offense while avoiding turnovers and tie-ups.

Improper footwork is the root of most turnovers. Pivot moves can turn players into human pretzels. A receiver will catch a pass and take an extra step to balance himself. A rebounder gets jittery after grabbing the ball and shuffles his feet. Good footwork leads to fewer turnovers and cuts way down on a coach's acid indigestion.

Pivots and Clear-Outs

We all know the deer-in-the-headlights look of the petrified player who has lost his dribble and stands clutching the ball near his belly button while waiting to be devoured by the defense. A tie-up or steal inevitably ensues. That's where pivots and clear-outs come charging to the rescue. They may not turn the deer into a lion, but they will provide some much-needed options for players who would normally feel helpless in such situations.

Being able to pivot and clear out the basketball gives any player a definite offensive advantage. Pivoting allows players to see the floor under pressure, stay in balance to avoid traveling violations, and make it extremely difficult for the defense to tie up or steal the basketball. Clear-out moves allow an offensive player to keep the ball away from even two defenders at a time while giving him time to find an open teammate. For ease of learning, break down these skills into two sections and then integrate them. During a game, they will be performed together.

Players can use four types of pivots. They can pivot forward or in reverse with either pivot foot (two pivot moves for each pivot foot). Players should start each pivot move with both feet shoulder-width apart and with both hands firmly on the basketball.

Footwork is the key to a pivot. To make a right front pivot, players establish the right foot as the pivot foot and then in one continuous motion they step the left foot forward in a semicircle, landing on the ball of the left foot (see figure 3.10). When this 180-degree turn is completed, both feet should be squared up in the opposite direction from where they started. To make a right reverse pivot, step the left foot backward until both feet are squared up in the opposite direction

For a left front pivot, players establish the left foot as the pivot foot, and then in one continuous motion they step the right foot forward in a semicircle and land on the ball of the right foot. When this 180-degree turn is completed, they should end with both feet squared up in the opposite direction from the starting position. For a left reverse pivot, players step the right foot backward in continuous motion until both feet are squared up in the opposite direction.

For younger players, coaches can teach a quarter-turn (90-degree) pivot, instead of a full 180-degree pivot. The important thing is to get the players to establish their pivot foot, and develop footwork that keeps the ball out of harm's way.

Once players master the pivot moves, they can then learn to execute two types of clear-outs: a high clear-out and a low clear-out. Clear-outs are executed with two hands on the ball. They are performed in combi-

Figure 3.10   To make a right front pivot and clear-out, a player establishes (*a*) the right foot as the pivot foot and holds the ball firmly in the hands, (*b*) steps the left foot around in a semicircle while sweeping the basketball through the face area, and (*c*) finishes with feet squared up in the opposite direction of the starting position.

nation with a pivot move and are designed to keep the ball away from opponents who are trying to steal or tie up the ball. Players should learn to clear out the ball every time they pivot. For both techniques, players should hold the ball firmly with both hands and sweep the ball with vigor. On a high clear-out, players sweep the basketball through the face area with an inverted-V motion as they pivot (see figure 3.10). On a low clear-out, players sweep the basketball through the knee area with a half-circle motion as they pivot.

Remind the players to keep their heads up while executing the pivot so they can see their teammates and make a quick pass. Balance is important, so make sure players keep their feet about shoulder-width apart during the pivot. If their feet are too wide or too close together, players risk tipping over while executing some of these moves. It's good for a few laughs in practice, but it'll cost them a traveling violation in a game. If nothing else, they should learn that they can't switch their pivot foot or they'll be called for a traveling violation.

Basket Cuts

The basket cut turns a player into a scoring threat. A player executing a basket cut aims to deceive and then fly past a defender. This skill is the basketball version of a Halloween trick *and* treat. The idea is for the offensive player to trick the defender into leaning in one direction and then cut to the basket the opposite way, where she should then be open to receive a pass from a teammate for an unguarded shot close to the rim (a treat on par with a family-sized chocolate bar).

How the cut is executed can make the difference between getting to the basket or being stopped short. To begin the basket cut, the player with the ball on the point passes it to either wing. After making the pass, the player makes a jab side step to the weak side (nonball side) of the court. Then the player moves toward the basket on the strong side (ball side) of the floor.

If the ball is passed to the right wing, the receiver jabs the left foot to the left (figure 3.11*a*), then quickly crosses the left foot back to the right and proceeds to the basket (figure 3.11*b*). If the ball was passed to the left wing, the receiver jabs with the right foot to the right, then crosses the right foot back to the left and proceeds to the basket. Ideally, the cut should be made down the lane through the gate area above the low block for the best angle to the basket. The cutter should keep his head up and hands out to receive a return pass.

This misdirection move is fundamental to offensive basketball. The basket cut teaches players how to move on the court without the ball. Moving in a straight line from one point to another is easy to defend. Offensive players should be encouraged to think of each movement as A to B

Figure 3.11   Players make basket cuts by making (*a*) jab side step in one direction and then (*b*) making a crossover step in the other direction to cut toward the basket.

to C: Start at A, make a jab side step one way to B, and cut the opposite way to C. This forces the defense to react in the "wrong" direction and gives the offensive player a split second of extra time to get open and create a clear passing lane to receive the ball from a teammate. Remind players to remember their ABCs as they practice this skill.

Setting Screens and Rolling

The screen and roll is an offensive play in which a player sets a screen and then rolls to the basket to receive a return pass for a score. When a player pulls off a screen and rolls for a shot—or, better yet, a basket—it's time to celebrate. That's when any coach knows that her group of youngsters is starting to perform like a team. It's one of the simplest teamwork skills to learn and also one of the most durable; the screen and roll has been the staple of many professional basketball team offenses for decades. Yet even first-year players can learn how to use it as an offensive weapon.

Setting a good screen is the basketball equivalent of stopping traffic so a friend can cross an intersection to safety. A screen blocks defenders to open a clear path to the basket for a teammate. The roll comes after a player sets a screen. The screener pivots toward the basket and opens up toward the ball to receive a pass. A screen and roll turns both players into a scoring threat and puts pressure on the defense.

There are countless ways to set and use screens, and it's a building block for just about any offensive set. Each screen uses similar skills. The screener should wave a hand toward a teammate and shout the teammate's name to alert the teammate a screen is on its way. The screener must set and hold position and should not move to block the defender. To set the screen, the screener should bend knees slightly, keep feet shoulder-width apart for balance, and hold the hands close to the body, with elbows in (see figure 3.12). The screener should be prepared for contact.

Figure 3.12 Correct body position for setting a screen.

Drill 1 Hand Speed Stationary Dribbling

🏀 BEGINNER

EQUIPMENT   A basketball for each player and one for the coach

PURPOSE   This drill develops hand speed for ballhandling and dribbling.

PROCEDURE   Have the players hold a ball and form a big circle around you as you demonstrate various dribbling exercises. For each exercise, the ballhandlers should first work on controlling the ball and then on building up their speed. Encourage the players to keep their heads up (control the ball without looking at it). They should bend at the knees, not the waist, with their butts low. Demonstrate each of the following exercises and then have the kids practice them.

- **Finger touch.** Control the ball by tipping it back and forth between the hands about one foot apart, using only fingertips. Move hands up and down as the drill proceeds.

- **Head, waist, and knees.** Wrap the ball around the head only, using both hands, and change directions. Wrap the ball around the waist only, using both hands, and change directions. Wrap the ball around the knees only (knees should be close to touching), using both hands, and change directions. Then move the ball down and up the body line (head, waist, knees, waist, head, and so on). Repeat several times.

- **Around each knee.** Wrap the ball around the right knee several times by handing the ball between right and left hands. Change directions. Then repeat around the left knee. Try to move the ball as quickly as possible without dropping it.

- **V dribble.** Bounce the ball from the left to the right hand in a V pattern. Make sure to bend the knees and keep the ball as low to the floor as possible. Have the opposite hand ready to catch the ball. Work on speed, keep the dribble sharp, and keep the head up.

If your players gain confidence with the first four exercises, you can add any of the modifications that follow. Far be it from us to recommend bribery, but certain incentives can go a long way toward pushing your ballhandlers in the right direction on these more challenging exercises: *If anyone can do this in the next two weeks, I'll get you ice cream*. If your budget can handle it, it's a great way to get the players psyched up about working on their hand speed.

FIGURE-EIGHT PATTERN WITHOUT DRIBBLE   Make a figure-eight pattern around both legs using both hands and no dribbles. The play-ers wrap the ball around the right leg at knee level with the right hand and then transfer the ball under the body to the left hand (see photo) to wrap around the left leg and continue the pattern as quickly as possible. The pattern can be completed front to back, or back to front.

STAGGERED DROP   Hold the ball in both hands between the legs, left arm in front of left leg and right arm behind right leg. Drop the ball and let it bounce once (see photo) then catch it by moving the right hand to the front and the left hand behind the left leg. Keep flipping hands in this manner for 20 seconds or more.

(continued)

⊕⊕⊕ ADVANCED VARIATIONS

STAGGERED FLIP Hold the ball in both hands between the legs, right arm behind the right leg and left arm in front. Drop the ball and catch it before it hits the ground by moving the right hand to the front and the left hand behind the left leg (see photo). Keep flipping hands in this manner for 20 seconds or more. Try to get at least five in a row without letting the ball drop to the floor.

TWO DRIBBLES ON THE RIGHT OR LEFT Players should dribble twice around the right leg with the right hand only. Feet should remain stationary, positioned slightly wider than shoulder width. Dribble the basketball next to the outside of the right leg (dribble 1), then bring the ball around the back of the right leg (see photo) and bounce it under the body by the inside of the right leg (dribble 2). The key is to move the right hand from behind the leg to the front of the leg in time to receive the ball off the bounce and continue the pattern. This drill can also be done on the left side. Most of your team will be right-handed, so this may seem impossible at first. Be patient. Demonstrate it, and encourage the players to work on it at home. Throw in another ice-cream bribe if things get desperate.

FIGURE-EIGHT PATTERN WITH DRIBBLE Players dribble around both legs using both hands and four dribbles. With the right hand, dribble (1) in front of the right foot, then wrap the ball around the body (see photo *a*) and between the legs; dribble (2) under the body, catching the ball with the left hand; dribble (3) with the left hand in front of the left foot; then wrap the ball around the body and between the legs; dribble (4) under the body (see photo *b*), catching it with the right hand. Begin the cycle again. If any player on your team masters this skill, have her report directly to the point guard position. Again, it's one to work on outside of practice.

Drill 2 Dribbling

🏀 BEGINNER

EQUIPMENT   Three basketballs

PURPOSE   In this drill players learn how to handle the basketball while moving down the court in simulated game conditions.

PROCEDURE   Form three lines on the baseline: one in the middle and one on each side nearer the sidelines. Give the first player in each line a ball. The first players in line dribble with the right hand straight down the court to the opposite baseline and then repeat on the way back. They hand the ball to the next player in line. After each player in line has completed his journey up and down the court, have the players dribble with the left hand straight down the court and back. Then have them try a crossover in a Z pattern (see figure): two dribbles to the right with the right hand, crossover dribble to the left hand, two dribbles to the left, and continue to the opposite baseline and back. The cuts need to be sharp to create a Z pattern. Dribblers can accomplish this by pushing off the outside foot in the direction of the ball on the crossover. While doing this, they should turn their shoulders in the direction they want to move.

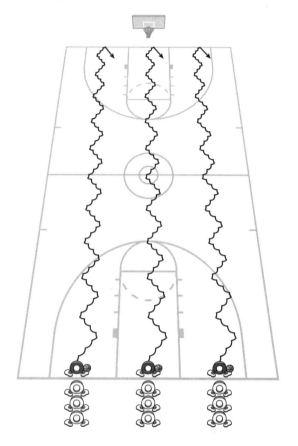

COACHING POINTS Have the players learn to control the ball, then work on speed. Players should keep their heads up and bend at the knees, not the waist. Work on getting everyone to dribble the ball at waist level or lower and to firmly snap the ball to the floor. On the crossover pattern, it's especially important to keep the ball low; this can be accomplished by keeping the receiving hand low and in position to receive the ball as it is transferred from the opposite hand. Dribblers should push off on the outside foot when crossing the ball over to the opposite hand. Players tend to meander down the court in a lazy S pattern. Emphasize that the crossover drill is not about speed up and down the court but about making sharp 45-degree cuts designed to elude an active defender.

Drill 3 Circle Up

EQUIPMENT   No basketballs are required

PURPOSE   This drill will help your players understand how to get their inside foot down first in relation to the basket. "Inside foot down first" is an important step toward building a great shot.

PROCEDURE   Players line up at the intersection of the baseline and the three-point line. Players move clockwise along the three-point line one after the other, about five feet apart. Each few steps, the players square up to the basket by placing the right or inside foot (the foot closest to the basket) down first and then bringing the opposite foot in line with it. By the time the players reach the other side of the baseline, they

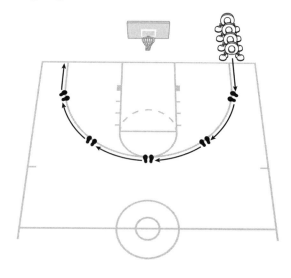

should complete four or five square-up moves. Once all the players have reached the other sideline, they line up again and execute the same series of square-ups in a counterclockwise direction along the three-point line. This time, their left foot will be the inside foot. Beginners should walk first, and then advance to a jog around the three-point line. When players grasp the footwork, add a simulated shot without the ball (shadow shot) to complete the drill.

COACHING POINTS   Make sure the players keep their heads level with eyes on the basket. Players' shoulders should be turned slightly toward the basket as they jog around the arc. Once they plant their inside foot, players should square up their feet and shoulders to the rim.

Drill 4 Pivoting

EQUIPMENT   Four basketballs

PURPOSE   This drill teaches offensive players to establish a pivot foot to avoid traveling violations and to use clear-outs to prevent tie-ups and turnovers.

PROCEDURE   Form four lines at the baseline and give a basketball to the first person in each line. The coach should be positioned at the midcourt line. On the coach's signal, all the players with a basketball take three dribbles toward the opposite baseline and come to a two-footed jump stop, squared up facing the opposite basket. Coach calls a three-pivot series: *Right front! Right reverse! Right front!* After completing

the series of three pivots, players snap a chest pass to the next player in line and return to the end of the line. On the next series, the coach should call out a different three-pivot series: *Left reverse! Left front! Left reverse!* Once players master the footwork, add clear-outs to the pivot moves to avoid turning the ball into a stationary target.

COACHING POINTS   The foot (right or left) that is called out is the foot that stays on the floor. After each pivot, the player's feet should be squared up and in balance. Make sure the player establishes and does not change the pivot foot throughout the series. The player should keep the head up while executing the pivot (*don't look at the feet, see the court*) and maintain balance. This drill is bound to create confusion at first, and many of the players will pivot off the wrong foot. If nothing else, they should learn that they can't switch their pivot foot, or else they'll be called for a traveling violation.

Drill 5 Step and Square

EQUIPMENT   No basketballs at first, then add a basketball for each player

PURPOSE   This drill teaches players how to square up to the basket for a shot by using proper footwork and body and arm position. This is a great starter drill because it is easy to set up, gets all the kids participating from the get-go, and is appropriate for all age levels.

PROCEDURE   Form two lines facing the basket starting at the two *elbows* (the intersections of the free-throw line and the lane lines). No basketballs are needed for the first part of the drill, but you'll add them as your team progresses to the additional steps. Players start on the elbows, keeping shoulders square to the backboard, and proceed to step down the lane line. Players alternate lines until they have proceeded down each lane line several times and mastered the footwork.

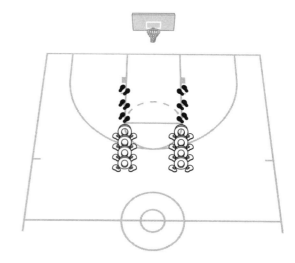

For the line on the right side (elbow at right free-throw lane line), players step with the left foot first, which is the "inside" foot, or the foot closest to the rim. As players step, they point the left foot at the basket. The right foot follows and squares up with the left foot. In the line on the left side (elbow at left free-throw line), the players step with the right foot first. As players step, they point the right foot at the basket. The left foot follows and squares up with the right foot.

COACHING POINTS   This drill focuses on footwork. As the players go through the drill, make sure they're putting the inside foot down first and watch carefully to make sure players square up the shoulders to the rim to match the position of their feet. Players will be tempted to pivot toward the rim after they put the inside foot down. This is not incorrect; it's just slower. If possible, they should learn to turn the foot before placing it on the floor so that they will be ready to take a shot even more quickly.

⛹⛹ INTERMEDIATE VARIATIONS

BALL PICKUP   Once players have the correct footwork, add a ball pickup to the drill. For the line on the right, players step down with the inside (left) foot first and dribble the ball once with the right hand. Placement of the dribble is important; it should be just in front of and slightly outside the right foot on the same side (right) of the dribbling hand. Then they pick up the ball off the dribble with both hands and bring it to the shot pocket (just above their waist) while they square up their feet to the basket. The players in the line on the left perform the same movements except they step down with the inside (right) foot and dribble once with the left hand.

COACHING POINTS   At first, the addition of the ball pickup will challenge many of the kids. They will tend to exaggerate the step and have difficulty coordinating the dribble. Have them shorten the step; this should help them sync it with the bounce of the ball.

LIFT AND BEND   When your team is ready, add a lift and bend (or coil) to the whole drill. Have the players line up at the elbows as before. The players in each line should complete the whole drill in sequence, adding the lift and bend just after the ball pickup.

COACHING POINTS   Always start with the ball in the shot pocket. Players tend to start with the ball too high—at chin level. Get them to start with it near their waist. The lift and bend should be simultaneous. Players should think *smooth*. Shooters should lift the ball so the index finger of the shooting hand comes to the chin–cheek area. The ball will pass in front of the face very briefly. Make sure the feet are squared up to the basket rim. If the feet are squared up, the shoulders will also be squared up.

Drill 6 Layups

EQUIPMENT No basketballs are required at first. Add them when players learn the footwork.

PURPOSE Most beginners will do just about anything to get the ball up to the basket. This drill will help them practice the proper footwork for shooting a layup.

PROCEDURE Players start without a basketball. No ball, no dribbling. Not yet. Each player approaches the basket from the right, through the gate, and completes a step and up. The player then moves to the left side of the basket and repeats the step and up. Once your players master the basic steps through the gate, add additional steps for the approach to the gate. From the right side, have them step left, right, left, and up. From the left, have them step right, left, right, and up. If they get the hang of this, add another two steps from each side. Then, repeat until they find the proper rhythm.

🏀🏀 **INTERMEDIATE VARIATION**

STEP AND UP WITH BASKETBALL When players understand the footwork, it's time to add the basketball, but no dribbling. Players should step through the gate from the right side with the basketball in both hands. Complete the footwork sequence and finish by shooting the ball with the right hand. Rebound the ball and repeat on the left side, shooting with the left hand. Continue to alternate sides.

COACHING POINTS Encourage the players to shoot with their weaker hand and use the proper footwork, even if they keep missing—and they'll miss a lot. Yes, Coach, your predominantly right-handed team will clank a lot of rightie layups at first and a lot more leftie layups. At this point, you smile and keep looking down . . . at your players' feet. Once the footwork clicks, everything else will catch up eventually.

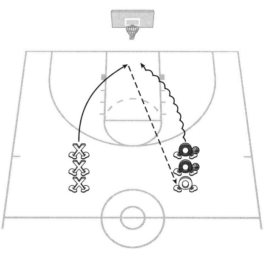

🏀🏀🏀 ADVANCED VARIATION

SHOOTING THE LAYUP

Now put it all together: Players dribble through the gate toward the basket and shoot a layup. Form a layup line on the right side of the half-court line facing the basket. Give balls to the first two or three players in this line. Form a rebound line on the left side of the half-court line facing the basket. The first player from the shooting line dribbles to the gate and shoots a layup and proceeds to the rebound line. The first player from the rebound line retrieves the ball and passes it to the first player without a ball in the shooting line and then the rebounder joins the shooting line.

COACHING POINTS   Make sure players are cradling the ball with both hands as they enter the gate area. They should bring the ball through the face area and lift toward the backboard. If they have built up enough speed on the way to the rim they should be able to shoot the layup with their shooting hand open and thumb out as the ball is released. Get the players in the mentality of attacking the basket: They should strive to get into the lane with purpose and go up strong toward the backboard with the ball. Emphasize *Game speed!* and *Do not be denied!* during the drill so that players go at the basket with urgency. They shouldn't feel like they can stroll to the rim and get off a shot in a game.

Drill 7 Give-and-Go

EQUIPMENT One basketball

PURPOSE This drill teaches players how to cut to the basket, shake loose from a defensive player, get open for a pass, and score. It's a great feeling for the players to see how working together can lead to a basket, and it's guaranteed to get them fired up. It might even prompt the most frazzled coach to break out in a grin. There's nothing like watching your players act like a team, and this drill is the first step toward teaching your players to think and act as a unit.

PROCEDURE Two lines form at the bottom corners of the lane, where the baseline meets the free-throw lane lines. A player from each line steps up to the low blocks, one with a ball, one without a ball. The player with the ball rolls it diagonally across the lane to the opposite elbow. The player who has rolled the ball chases it and picks it up at about the elbow (see *a*). This may require a few practice rolls so your players can figure out how fast or slow they need to roll the ball in order to catch up with it at the proper spot.

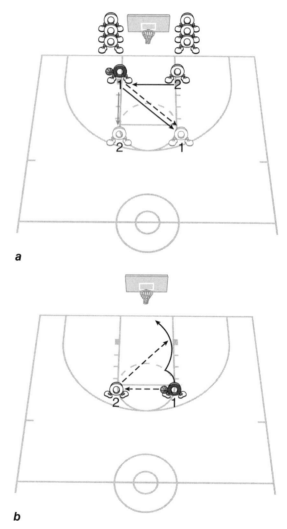

Once the ball starts rolling, the player without the ball runs to the opposite low block, pushes off her outside foot, and cuts up to the elbow along the outside of the free-throw lane line (*a*). Both players should be at or near their respective elbows once the ball is retrieved. The player who picks up the ball passes it to the other player on the opposite elbow (see *b*). The passer then cuts down the lane. The receiver catches the pass and immediately passes back to the player cutting to the basket, who then shoots a layup.

COACHING POINTS   Once again, footwork is the key. The player should roll the ball fast enough to chase it down without moving far beyond the free-throw line. Players should cut by pushing off the outside foot (the foot opposite the direction the player wants to move). Players should run in straight lines and cut at 90-degree angles. Emphasize crisp passes (chest or bounce passes). Younger players can finish the sequence by landing on both feet simultaneously and shooting a short shot off the backboard instead of a layup.

Drill 8 Basket Cutting

⊕⊕ INTERMEDIATE

EQUIPMENT   No basketball at first, then add a basketball

PURPOSE   This drill is meant to teach players how to move without the ball and get in position to score.

PROCEDURE   Form two lines about 10 feet apart above the free-throw lane at the three-point line, facing the basket. A coach or player steps out on each wing with a basketball. Players jab-sidestep in the opposite direction they want to cut. They then cut toward the ball side (strong side) down the lane, proceeding through the gate area (see *a*).

No pass is made at first to allow players to master the basket-cut footwork. After players master the footwork, the players at the top of the key should start with a ball. They start the drill by making a pass to the wing (see *b*). Then, the point players jab-sidestep and cut to the strong side. Finally, they receive a return pass from the wing and shoot a layup or a jump-stop layup.

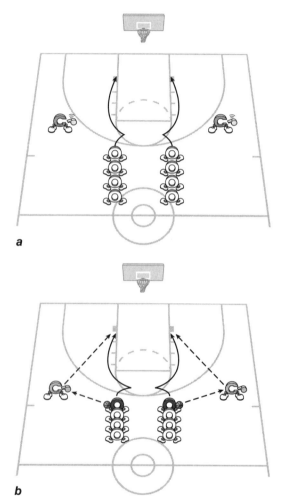

a

b

COACHING POINTS   Players should use the foot opposite the pass to jab-sidestep and cut. Make sure they keep their hands out to give the passer a target and receive a return pass. Make sure the cutter concentrates on one thing at a time by maintaining a controlled pace. You want quick movements, not frantic ones. Players must concentrate on catching the ball first by looking the ball into their hands, then focusing on the shot once the ball is secure. Emphasize that players should go through the gate for the best angle to the basket.

Drill 9 Two Balls on the Block

◎◎INTERMEDIATE

EQUIPMENT   Two basketballs

PURPOSE   Players doing this activity will learn to shoot on both sides of the basket, enhance strength and conditioning, and improve their footwork. This is a great starter drill for getting kids used to the idea of going up strong near the rim. In games these types of close-in shots will be contested by defenders and there will be a lot of bumping and jostling for position.

PROCEDURE   Place three players at each available basket and place a basketball on each low block next to the basket. The shooter lines up between the two balls. Two rebounders line up on opposite low blocks. The shooter reaches down and picks up the ball on the right side and makes a shot off the right side of the backboard. After the shot, the player proceeds to the left-side low block, picks up the ball, and makes a

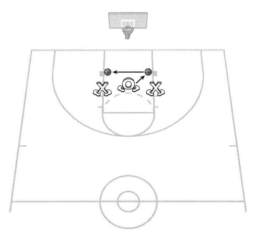

shot off the left side of the backboard. After each shot, the rebounders retrieve the ball and place it back on the low block. The drill continues for 30 to 60 seconds. Kids should keep track of how many baskets they score in the allotted time.

COACHING POINTS   Remind rebounders that they must return the ball to the low block, not hand the ball to the shooter. Emphasize that the shooter must go up strong, preferably off two feet for added power. Rushing through the drill will only lead to missed shots, so players should strive to maintain good form. Players will miss if they don't use a proper shooting angle. Have players strive to shoot from a 45-degree angle to the basket, which enables the shooter to take full advantage of the backboard for improved accuracy.

Drill 10 Screen and Roll

⚀⚀⚀ ADVANCED

EQUIPMENT One basketball, when players are ready

PURPOSE Screening takes players a step closer to being a team. This drill will help a young team learn the basics of setting a screen and see how it can be applied to scoring a basket.

PROCEDURE Place offensive players in a triangle above the three-point line (point, right wing, left wing) with no basketball at first. A token defender covers the right wing. The point player simulates a pass to the left-wing player. After the simulated pass, the point player sets a screen on the right-wing defender. The screener alerts teammates with a hand gesture and verbal prompt that a screen is being set (calling out the name of the player the screen is set for). The right-wing player cuts or curls over the top of the screen to the basket and prepares to receive a pass from the left-wing player. The cutter should think *ABC*: jab-sidestep in the opposite direction they want to go to cut around the screen. Once players understand how to set the screen, add a basketball.

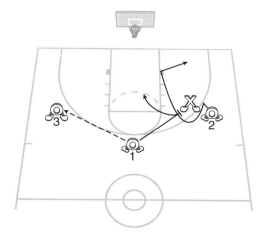

COACHING POINTS Make sure screeners set and hold position; they need to be balanced, with knees slightly bent and feet shoulder-width apart. They cannot shuffle their feet, or they will be called for a blocking foul (moving screen). Encourage the verbal and nonverbal communication between the screener and cutter as the screen is being set.

⚀⚀⚀ ADVANCED VARIATION

SCREEN AND ROLL When players have learned how to set the screen, add a roll. After the right-wing player (2) cuts over the top of the screen to the basket and clears the lane, the screener (1) opens to the ball and rolls to the basket. The left-wing player (3) then passes to the screener rolling to the basket. Simulate the passes when first adding this modification. When players understand the movements, add a ball.

COACHING POINTS Once the offensive player has set the screen, have the screener pivot toward the basket and open up to the ball. Timing is important; the screener should roll after the first cutter has cleared the lane.

The Coach's Clipboard

✔ Teach the players how to pass, but don't overlook the catch.

✔ Build hand speed with stationary ballhandling drills.

✔ Emphasize dribbling with either hand.

✔ Teach your team how to get good shots; the baskets will follow.

✔ Layups win games. Missed layups lose games.

✔ Players need to get involved in the offense even when they don't have the ball by cutting to the basket and setting screens.

✔ Great shooting starts with great footwork.

✔ Pivoting and clearing out the ball prevent tie-ups and turnovers.

✔ Offensive players don't move in straight lines; they jab-sidestep in one direction, then cut in the opposite direction.

✔ The screen and roll and the give-and-go are stepping stones to offensive teamwork.

Teaching Defensive Skills With 10 Simple Drills

This is where a coach's powers of persuasion are really put to the test. Let's face it: defense isn't as much fun as offense. Defense means hard work and discipline, and discipline is defined in one dictionary as "training to act in accordance with rules; drill." Ugh.

Discipline and hard work aren't traits that most kids come by naturally. This is where the coach needs not only to teach, but to motivate. Kids may not understand the need for discipline and rules, but they can relate to energy and hustle. A lot of your players may not know or care about the difference between man-to-man and zone, but many of them will love to run, jump, and dive on the floor for loose objects, including basketballs. You can channel that energy into great defense. So let's add another "d" word besides discipline to our defensive lexicon: *desire*.

Here's the carrot at the end of the stick: defense is a way for the kid who isn't a scoring star to make a huge impact on the outcome of a game. Make it clear from the first practice that shut-down defenders are every bit as valuable to the team as prolific scorers. Praise and reward great defensive play in practice and in games. Make it clear that defense is a priority every bit as important as scoring baskets. Remember, if the other team can't score, you can't lose.

Rules for Contact

Good defense requires a certain amount of body contact with the opponent. But there is an appropriate time for such contact, and a time when too much physical stuff will get a defender in serious foul trouble. Early on, explain to your eager young defenders what type of contact is permissible on a basketball court and what type violates the rules or could potentially injure an opponent. There's a time to muscle up on defense, and a time to back off and shadow your opponent.

In general, when your opponent has the ball, no touching—or shoving, pushing, nudging, or reaching for that matter—is allowed. When your opponent is moving without the ball or getting in position for a rebound, more physical contact is permitted, but within limits. Make clear the difference between using an *arm bar* to block an opponent's path or box out for a rebound, which is permitted in basketball, and throwing an elbow, which is not. An arm bar is created by locking out the forearm and using it to block an opponent's path. The arm or elbow should never be swung in the direction of an opponent. Accidents—and the occasional bloody nose—happen because of overzealous defense, so it's important to emphasize that there are limits and rules, and referees to oversee them.

Footwork is a foundation of good defense, and coaches should encourage defenders to rely on their feet to stay ahead of the player they are covering. But defenders also need to keep their hands to themselves. Warn them from the get-go not to reach for the ball in the open court. Once in a while, a reach produces a steal. But more often it will result in a slap of the ballhandler's wrist or a handful of air. The defender who reaches throws himself off balance and gives the ballhandler an opportunity to drive to the basket. A reach is also the quickest way to pick up an unnecessary foul. The reach-in foul is one of the most common in basketball because it is easy to spot by a referee. Bottom line: reaching is bad basketball.

Stance and Positioning

Good defense starts with a proper stance. Without it as a base, a defender won't be able to move quickly enough to stop an opponent driving to the basket. There are three basic defensive stances, which depend on the defender's relationship to the ball. That relationship will change each time the ball moves on the court, either via pass or dribble.

It's important for a good defensive player to master all three stances, but mastery is a process that can take years. So don't start pulling your hair out just yet. Start with the basic stance, and then slowly start massaging into your players' heads how that stance will be slightly modified depending on where the ball is on the court.

On the Ball   The basic on-the-ball stance applies to any defensive situation. Many young players tend to bend over from the waist, throwing off their balance. Instead, encourage them to bend at the knees, keepings their butts low. Feet should be spread a little wider than shoulder width (see figure 4.1). Both arms should be spread to either side, elbows slightly bent, thumbs up.

When covering the player with the ball, the defender must keep his nose on the ball. The goal is to cut off the ballhandler's path to the basket, no matter which direction the offensive player moves. Players should not reach for the ball; they should keep their arms spread to the side with the elbows bent, and move the arms in short tight circle patterns to generate momentum in the desired direction to stay ahead of the ball.

Figure 4.1   On-the-ball stance.

Deny   The deny stance applies when defending an offensive player who is in immediate proximity to the ball or one pass away. The defender should position himself between his opponent and the basket and stay low by bending at the knees (see figure 4.2). The defender denies the pass by extending his outside hand (hand closest to the passer) into the passing lane with palm open, thumb down. The defender should turn his head slightly over his shoulder so that he can see the ball along with the offensive player he is guarding.

Figure 4.2   Deny stance.

Open   For defenders who are not covering the ballhandler and are more than one pass away from the ball, an open, or help, stance is a must. This requires that defenders move to the *help line*—the imaginary line that splits the court in half from basket to basket—and turn their backs to the basket they're defending. They should have arms spread and knees bent (see figure 4.3). Defenders are part of an imaginary triangle that includes the offensive player being guarded and the player with the ball: Ball, you, man. Defenders should be able to point to the ball with one outstretched hand and the player they're guarding with the other hand.

One of the most common mistakes of young defenders at the help line is to turn their shoulders so that they see only the ball side (strong side) of the court or their assigned player moving without the ball. Either way, they can't see something important: the ball, or their man. But with back turned to the basket in an open stance, they can see the whole court. Unlike the on-the-ball stance, where the defender is focused on staying in front of the ball, the open stance allows the defender to use her peripheral vision to react quickly to the movement of the ball or movement of opponents away from the ball cutting toward the basket.

Figure 4.3   A defender who is more than one pass away from the ball (player at far right) should move to an open, or help, stance.

Player Movement

Good defense depends on moving quickly *under control*. Once players sprint back into half-court defensive position, they won't be running much anymore. Instead, they'll be using slide steps and close-outs. These movements require discipline and repetition to master—traits not normally associated with preadolescent athletes. But your defense will improve as your players learn that running pell-mell is not the best way to slow down an opponent's scoring.

Slide Step With Drop Step
Defenders mostly move side to side while defending the basket. The slide step requires short, choppy steps; the feet should not touch or cross but slide to cut off the ballhandler and force him to change direction. As the ballhandler changes direction, so must the defender. To change direction from right to left, the defender should drop (step back with) the left foot and then slide. To change direction from left to right, the defender drops (steps back with) the right foot and then slides. If necessary to stay ahead of the ballhandler, who has suddenly changed direction, the defender can briefly sprint back to catch up and get ahead, then resume slide-stepping.

The defender aims to keep moving so that her head and nose are always on the basketball. The defender's body should be lined up opposite the basketball instead of directly in front of the ballhandler, slightly offsetting the defender's body from the offensive player so that the defender is always ahead of the ball. By staying ahead of the ball in this way, the defender forces the ballhandler to "turn" away from his preferred route to the basket. Of course, to maintain this position against a ballhandler desperate to penetrate the lane and look for a score requires the defender to work hard. You will hear coaches urging on their defenders: *Work for position* and *Turn him, turn him*. At first, rookie defenders may find this task difficult. It requires tenacity and a certain attitude: *You aren't getting past me no matter how fast you dribble!*

Many of your players won't be accustomed to having to work this strenuously for something that seems relatively thankless. So recognize the effort: Every time a defender slide-steps and makes the ballhandler turn or stop dribbling out of frustration, applaud the defender. Bulldog defenders are often unsung stars on teams. Make sure they are sung about often on your team.

Close-Out   It's important for a defender to learn how to close the distance between himself and an offensive player who has just received the ball and is a threat to dribble, pass, or shoot. The defender should approach quickly but under control, with a shuffle step or stutter step to slow down. She must also stay low and maintain her defensive stance with an arm up to match the shooting hand of the offensive player (left hand up for right-hand shooter) to discourage the outside shot (figure 4.4).

Figure 4.4   Closing out.

The defender should stop about three feet away from the offensive player, otherwise the offensive player will be able to dribble around the defender. Staying low will enable the defender to drop-step and stay with the offensive player who begins to dribble toward the basket. Above all, the defender who closes out must defend the layup first. If there is a choice between leaving a little extra room to defend against the drive and squeezing the offensive player a little tighter to discourage the jump shot, always guard against the drive.

Jumping to the Ball   Every time the offense passes the ball, each defensive player must react and "jump" to the ball while it is still in the air. This involves a combination of slide steps and close-outs, depending on where the defenders are in relation to the ball. The defender covering the new ballhandler must close out. The other defensive players must slide-step into deny or open (help) position, depending on their proximity to the ball. By slide-stepping, rather than turning their shoulders and walking or running into position, the defenders keep their backs turned to their basket and can see both their man and the ball at all times.

Rebounding

Holding the other team's offense to no shots, or one shot, is the standard of great defense. So getting a rebound off a missed shot is the last, crucial element in any defensive stand. Kids who get rebounds should get plenty of back-slaps and high fives for a job well done. The defender who scraps for every loose ball should be showered with praise. Rebounding requires a certain mindset and facial expression—an expression that says, *Grrrr!* Feel free to demonstrate this game-face look, Coach. If nothing else, the kids should get a good laugh as they get in the proper mood.

Rebounders must catch the ball with arms extended overhead. They should jump to meet the ball as high as they can rather than waiting for it to fall to head or shoulder level. To add explosiveness to their leap, rebounders should crouch slightly, then extend arms while they jump. Encourage players to go and get the ball. Many fledgling rebounders stand underneath the basket with hands raised and knees locked out, as if praising the heavens and waiting for the ball to drop to them. Raised hands and locked knees don't add much to a player's leaping ability, so have the players think about getting wider and creating space for themselves to jump as high as possible.

After the rebound is made, make sure the ball is secured with two hands, with elbows slightly out, and that it remains at or above head level. The ball should be grasped toward the front of the body; don't place the basketball toward the back of the head because this will allow a defender to snatch the ball from behind.

In the battle for the rebound, the players who box out the best will usually wind up with the ball. *Butt in the gut*—that's the best way to describe the technique required to box out an opponent. The rebounder's hands should move to create a small box behind the rebounder to seal the opponent away from the basket (figure 4.5). The rebounder should use hands to feel an opponent's direction, then reverse pivot to seal off the opponent. Here's the coach's mantra to every rebounder: Find the opponent's body, then find the ball.

Figure 4.5   Boxing out an opponent.

Defending the Cutter

Offenses run wild when players without the basketball can cut from the weak side through the lane to receive passes and create close-range shots. Defenders must learn to block or divert cutters *before* the pass arrives. This is called *cutting the cutter*.

The defender should create an arm bar with the forearm to block the opponent's progress (see figure 4.6) and force the offensive player to change direction away from the basket. The arm bar should be made with the arm closest to the cutter. The elbow should be bent and the defender should use the forearm to block the cutter's path. The defender's outside arm (closest to the ball) goes up to deny a pass to the cutter. The defensive player should prepare for contact and keep balance by bending the knees and widening the stance slightly: get lower and wider. Making physical contact with the cutter is a must. Otherwise, there's no need for the cutter to stop. Get the players used to this idea in practice. The cutter should feel the defender's determination.

Figure 4.6 Proper technique to stop a cutter.

Defending the Post

Teaching young players how to defend a player who wants the basketball in close to the basket is another challenge. It requires defenders to get even more up close and personal with their opponents. Remember the old Olivia Newton-John song, "Physical," as in "Let's get physical"? Get that boombox ready, Coach, because that song should be the sound-track for this drill.

Most post players position themselves in the low post, just above the low block and outside the lane (to avoid a three-second violation). If they position themselves at the free-throw line elbow, this is the high post. A post player positioned in between is in the mid-post area.

At the younger age levels, mid-post and high-post defense can be accomplished using the close-out technique described earlier in this chapter. Doing so prevents the post player from being able to dribble to the basket for a layup. If the post player dribbles and then picks up the dribble, the defender should "belly up" to make a shot or pass difficult. Defending the player who sets up with back turned to the basket to receive an entry pass in the low post requires defenders to know how to handle the following situations.

- **Entry pass to the post.** A defender can deny the entry pass to the post by extending the arm closest to the ball into the passing lane, thumb down, and creating an arm bar with the opposite arm to lean against the post player (see figure 4.7). To make the entry pass even more difficult, the defender also can step into the passing lane with the foot closest to the ball. This defensive tactic will be used when the basketball is being entered from the point or wing area of the court.

Figure 4.7   Defender denying an entry pass to the low post.

- **Pass to the corner.** If the ball is passed to the corner, the defender must "step through" and then deny the pass. A step-through is a two-step footwork sequence. The defender steps through the passing lane in front of the post player (see figure 4.8*a*), then turns 180 degrees and denies the entry pass (figure 4.8*b*). The defender is in position to block or intercept any pass to the corner and to discourage a drive from the baseline. When the basketball is passed back to the wing or to the point, the defender must step back into the deny defensive stance, with the body between the offensive player and the basket and outside hand extended into the passing lane.

Figure 4.8   When denying a pass from the corner, a defender (*a*) steps through the passing lane and (*b*) then turns 180 degrees to deny the pass.

- **Size advantage.** To defend a player with a size advantage in the low post, a defender can "front" the post (see figure 4.9). The defensive player stands in front of the low-post player to prevent other players from being able to enter a bounce or chest pass into the low post. Fronting the post requires balance and footwork because the defender cannot see the post player. But it forces the offense to attempt a risky lob pass to get the ball to the post. If the offense attempts the lob, the post defender must have help from a weak-side defender to "sandwich" the low-post player.

Figure 4.9 Defender fronting a low post with a size advantage.

Drill 1 Ready, Set, Defense

EQUIPMENT   None

PURPOSE   This drill reinforces the proper stance needed for good defensive play.

PROCEDURE   Players form a circle (or line up on the length of one sideline) and maintain the proper defensive stance position for several short time sequences. Make a little game out of this drill to see who can hold the best defensive stance the longest. Coach shouts, "Ready, set, defense!" Players assume the stance and hold it for as long as possible or until Coach blows the whistle. The player who holds it the longest or exhibits the best form then gets a turn to shout, "Ready, set, defense!" for the next round.

COACHING POINTS   Defenders should bend knees slightly and get butts down. They need to stay low for quick lateral movement. Make sure arms are spread wide, elbows slightly bent. Players should not stand up or straighten knees while holding the stance.

Drill 2 Z Slides

🏀 BEGINNER

EQUIPMENT   None

PURPOSE   This drill teaches defenders to stay in front of the ballhandler and cut off the path to the basket.

PROCEDURE   Players line up in one line on the right side of the baseline with their backs facing the court. In turn, each player slides sideways and moves backward down the floor in a "Z" pattern. Use a drop step to change direction: slide two steps to the right, drop left foot and slide two steps to the left (and down the court), then drop the right foot and slide two steps to the right, and so on. When each player reaches half-court, the next player begins to slide and drop. At the opposite baseline, players move to the left half of the court and work their way backward down the floor on the left side. Go slowly at first until players master the technique of slid-

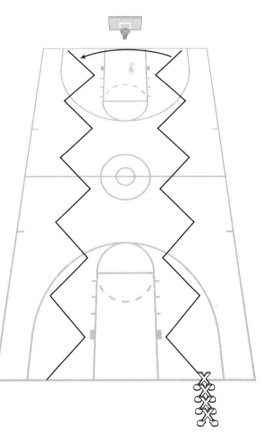

ing. Otherwise, practice will quickly turn into a slapstick routine with lots of would-be defenders landing on their fannies.

COACHING POINTS   Defenders need to work on staying low and maintaining stance all the way down the floor. They should use short, choppy steps; their feet should not touch or cross. When changing direction from right to left, the defender should drop the left foot. When changing direction from left to right, the defender should drop the right foot.

Drill 3 Close-Outs

🏀 BEGINNER

EQUIPMENT   A basketball for the defensive line

PURPOSE   Practicing this drill will teach players to close ground and defend against a triple-threat offensive player (who can dribble, shoot, or pass). The main goal is to prevent the offensive player from driving around and scoring a layup, but the defender must also discourage an outside shot.

PROCEDURE   Form two lines (defense) at the intersections of the baseline and the free-throw lane lines. Form two more lines (offense) at the elbows. Each defender at the baseline passes the ball to the offensive player at the elbow on the same side and then closes out the offensive player.

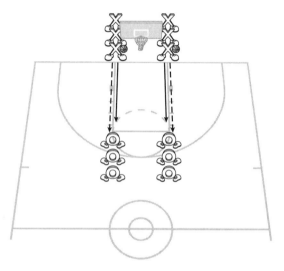

COACHING POINTS   Defenders should stutter-step to slow down and stay balanced on final approach. Listen for the squeak of the gym shoes. Cup your hand to your ear, and the kids will quickly get the message: The louder the squeak, the better the technique. Watch that the defender maintains proper distance—about the length of an arm and a half—to cut off the drive and discourage the outside shot. The defender should raise a hand to contest the shot and stay low, ready to move.

Drill 4 Foot-Fire

🏀 BEGINNER

EQUIPMENT   Basketball

PURPOSE   This drill encourages defenders to keep their feet moving, emphasizes the value of the close-out, and is great for conditioning.

PROCEDURE   Form three parallel lines about 10 feet apart, with an equal number of players in each line, down the length of the court. Players in each line should be about 3 feet behind the player in front of them. Players in the two outside lines face the player opposite them in the middle line. The coach should be positioned at the top of the middle line with a basketball. The players in the middle line start the drill facing the coach. They should be in a defensive stance with their arms out, thumbs up, and knees bent.

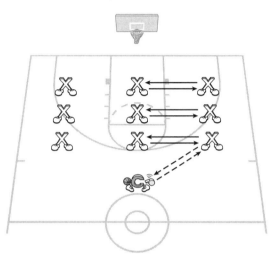

On the coach's command, the middle line moves their feet up and down rapidly, as if running in place but without lifting knees as high. The footwork should be short, quick, and rapid-fire. Players continue foot-fire until the coach passes the ball to the front player in one of the outside lines. While the ball is in the air, players in the middle line move to close out their counterparts in the line that will receive the pass. Players hold close-out position until the coach has had a chance to evaluate each player's stance. The coach then calls for the ball, and players return to their original positions. Foot-fire continues, with the coach alternating the side to which the basketball is passed.

After five or six sequences, lines switch places until all three lines have been in the middle. At first, there will be lots of giggling during this drill; when the giggling stops, you'll know the kids are tired and it's time to switch lines. Keep the drill moving so that none of the lines are waiting too long for action.

COACHING POINTS   Encourage players to move their feet as rapidly as possible: short, choppy, quick. Defenders must close out to a safe distance (2 to 3 feet) and maintain proper stance.

Drill 5 Sky High

EQUIPMENT   Basketball

PURPOSE   Rebounders practice securing a missed shot to give their team possession of the basketball.

PROCEDURE   The coach stands with a basketball on the left side of the rim. Rebounders line up on the right side of the rim. The coach tosses the ball to the opposite side of the rim off the backboard (without touching the rim), and the rebounder jumps to catch the ball with arms extended overhead. The rebounder should try to catch the ball as high as possible overhead and

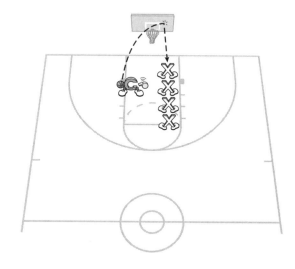

then return the ball to the coach. The procedure is repeated for each person in line until each player has rebounded several times. This drill should move quickly.

COACHING POINTS   Players should catch the ball with arms extended and work to keep the ball high and in front of the head.

⊛⊛⊛ ADVANCED VARIATION

BOXING OUT Catching the ball is only part of effective rebounding. Equally critical is boxing out. Once players have developed a feel for catching the ball off the backboard, they can begin working on establishing position against another player. Put three defenders at the baseline about four to five feet apart, and spread three offensive players about the same distance apart across the free-throw

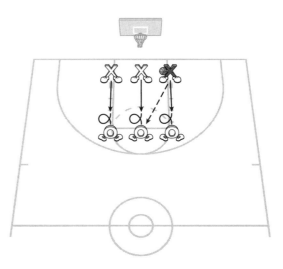

line. Give a basketball to one of the defenders.

The defender with the ball passes it to one of the offensive players. The three defenders move to close out each of the offensive players. The defenders should allow the player who has the ball to take a shot. After the shot is launched, defenders extend their hands to meet their opponents and determine which way the offensive players want to move toward the basket. The defenders then reverse pivot to box out their opponent in this direction. Once the opponent is sealed away from the basket, each defender then releases and goes after the ball.

COACHING POINTS The defensive rebounders must make contact with offensive players, reverse pivot, and work for butt-in-the-gut positioning before going for the ball. The drill cannot be completed without physical contact.

Drill 6 Wing Deny

EQUIPMENT   Basketball

PURPOSE   This drill gives players practice in defending against a player who is moving to the wing or who is already out on the wing and awaiting a pass from the point. Defenders learn how to position themselves to deny the pass even as the wing player moves to get free.

PROCEDURE   The offensive player and one defender start on the low block on the free-throw lane. Add a coach with a basketball at the top of the key to more accurately reflect game conditions. The offensive player (without the ball) moves to the wing 15 to 18 feet from the basket and back down to the low block. As the wing player moves back and forth, the defender main-

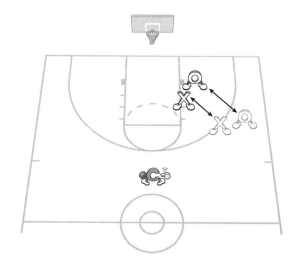

tains proper stance while sliding to stay between the wing player and the basket.

As players learn footwork, a point player or coach can try to pass to the wing player. Offensive players should not make any elaborate moves to try to elude the defender. The offensive player must go to the assigned spots so the defensive player can learn proper technique and foot skills. As the season proceeds and defenders become more proficient at denying the wing player, the coach at the top of the key can start attempting to pass to the wing to ensure that the defender is always aware of where the ball is.

COACHING POINTS   Defenders must work on staying low and must never stand up or lock out the knees. They should always strive to keep their body between the offensive player and the basket, while extending a hand into the passing lane. It's especially critical to remind defenders where they should be looking: They need to turn the head slightly to see the ball, while still seeing their man.

Drill 7 Help Defense

EQUIPMENT Basketball

PURPOSE Running this drill helps players practice reacting to a pass and assuming the proper position to "help" teammates defend the ball.

PROCEDURE Begin with two offensive players (one with the ball on point and one on the wing) and one defender on point. Tell the kids the wing is being covered by an imaginary defender. When the ball is passed from the point to the wing, the defender jumps to the ball with a hop step and without running all the way over to cover the wing. The defender is now positioned between the ball and his man where he can see both, which is the proper "help" position in relation to ball. The defender should put a hand in the passing lane.

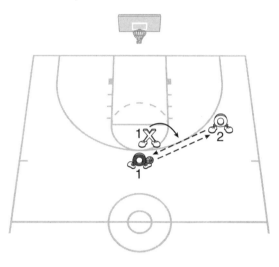

95

Drill 8 Tandem Defense

EQUIPMENT Basketball

PURPOSE This drill helps players learn the concept of working together to protect the basket and close out a shooter, providing a foundation for team defense that you'll teach them later (see chapter 6). The skills learned in this drill can also be used as an effective way to slow down or shut down a fast-break offense.

PROCEDURE Begin with three offensive players (point and two wings) and two defenders. The offensive player at point starts with the ball. One defender lines up at the free-throw line to defend the point. The second defender lines up 10 feet directly behind the first defender in basket protection at the help line. The point defender must be ready to slide-step, while the basket-protection defender is in an open stance to see both sides of the floor. To begin, walk through each of the positions so that players understand the concept of basket protection and body position, then work slowly up to game speed.

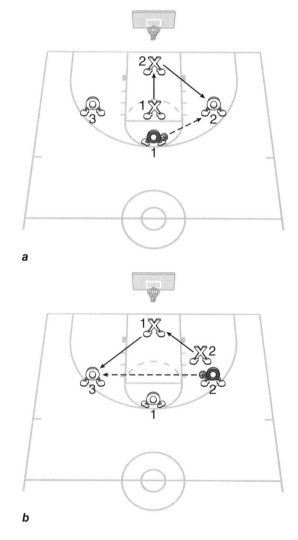

On a pass from the point to either wing, the basket defender covers the first pass to either wing by closing out the wing who receives the pass. The point defender drops straight back to assume the basket-protection position (see *a*). On a pass back to the point, both defenders return to their original positions: The basket defender moves up to defend the point and the wing defender moves to basket protection. On a pass from one wing to the opposite wing (skip pass), the defender in basket protection moves to defend and close out the wing receiving the pass, and the other defender moves to basket protection (this is known as a tandem shift; see *b*). If the wing who received the skip pass passes to the point, the defender in basket protection moves up, and the tandem wing defensive player moves to basket protection.

COACHING POINTS   Defenders must maintain an open stance as they drop back so they can see both sides of the court at all times. Emphasize that the two defenders can't necessarily stop three offensive players from shooting or even scoring, but they are trying to prevent the easy layup. They can also work to force as many passes as possible so that in a similar game situation their teammates would have time to get back and help defend.

Drill 9 Cut the Cutter

EQUIPMENT   Basketball

PURPOSE   This drill helps defenders practice disrupting offensive cutters to prevent the offense from creating easy baskets in the lane.

PROCEDURE   Start with one offensive player at the point with a ball and another offensive player at the wing. On the opposite wing, create a line of offensive players outside the threepoint line. One defensive player lines up in deny position to defend the first wing player. The point and the opposite wing player are not defended.

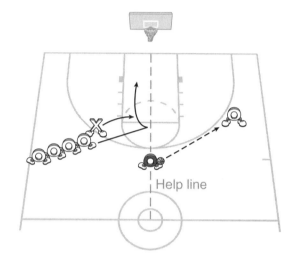

Help line

The point passes to the unguarded wing player. On the pass, the defensive player jumps to the ball and arrives with an open stance at the help line in the middle of the lane. The defender's outside arm (closest to the ball) goes up to deny the pass to the cutter, and the defender's opposite arm (closest to the cutter) creates an arm bar to prevent the cut. Walk through this part of the drill so that players develop the proper technique and position. After the defender jumps to the ball, rotate players: The player in the cutter line moves to defense, the defender moves to the unguarded wing, the wing moves to the point, and the point moves to the back of the cutter line.

When players are ready, begin working on cutting the cutter. After the point passes to the unguarded wing, the weak-side cutter tries to cut over the top of the defensive player to get in position for a pass from the wing. The defensive player puts up an arm bar and forces the cutter to move away from the free-throw lane area.

COACHING POINTS   Defenders should stay low and balanced and get an arm bar up. Body contact between defender and cutter is a must. Encourage the players to get physical but to avoid swinging an elbow that could hurt the cutter. Tell the players to think of the arm bar as a wall, not a weapon.

Drill 10 Shell

EQUIPMENT   Basketball

PURPOSE   This drill reinforces the concepts of jumping to the ball, moving to the help line, closing out, putting a hand in the passing lane, and staying open to the ball.

PROCEDURE   Begin with four defensive players: two on opposite low blocks and two at opposite elbows. These positions are the "home" position for the defenders. Five offensive players start around the perimeter: one at point, two on opposite wings, and two in opposite corners. The point guard's job is to rotate the ball to the opposite side of the court, so for this drill, the point guard should not be covered by a defender.

When the ball is at the point, the defensive players are in their "home" position (see *a*). On a pass from the point to the wing, the defenders should move on the flight of the ball to coverage areas (*b*). The defender closest to the wing should close out. The defender closest to the strong-side corner player should move to deny a

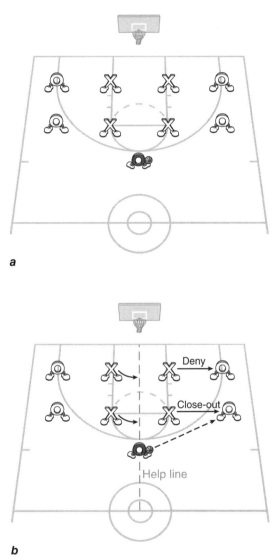

a

b

(continued)

pass to the corner. Defenders at the weak-side elbow and weak-side low block must move to the help line. On a pass from the wing to the strong-side corner, the defenders should move on the flight of ball (*c*). The strong-side corner defender closes out. The strong-side wing defender denies a return pass to the wing. The weak-side defenders slide to the help line.

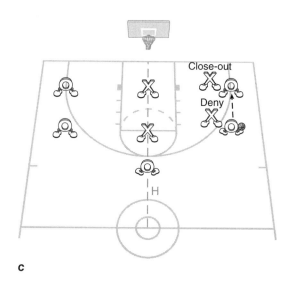

c

Start slowly by passing the basketball from point to wing to corner around the perimeter. Don't allow any skip passing across the court yet. Give the players a chance to react to the basketball. Defenders need to understand that they must adjust their physical relationship to their man and to the ball with every pass. Each time the ball moves, they need to move—and fast. When defenders jump to the ball, and the offense will find it that much harder to penetrate the defense and score easy baskets. Defenders should be communicating. If on the ball: *Ball!* If in deny: *Deny!* If in help defense: *Help!*

For beginners, the offensive players should pause for a few counts before making the next pass. As players learn the drill, increase the speed. Once players learn to quickly adjust to the ball movement, allow skip passing to all points of the floor. Skip passing will give more of a game-type feel to the drill. Defenders should *not* attempt to intercept or impede any pass. The focus should be on reacting to ball movement and realigning themselves during each pass.

COACHING POINTS Defenders must jump to the ball on each pass. Pass receivers should be closed out. All defenders must stay open to the ball and also the weak side of the floor. Defenders who are one pass away should deny the pass. Remaining defenders who are more than one pass away should be at the help line.

The Coach's Clipboard

✔ Desire, hustle, and energy trump talent on defense.

✔ Defenders need to get tough—but within limits.

✔ Quick feet, not reaching hands, are the foundation of great defense.

✔ Help defenders need to stay open to the ball.

✔ Man-to-man defenders must slide-step and drop-step to stay ahead of the ball.

✔ Close-outs are the key to defending the offensive player who has just caught a pass.

✔ Every time the offense passes, defenders should jump to the ball.

✔ Butt in the gut is the key to gaining rebound position.

✔ Use the forearm as an arm bar to cut the cutter.

✔ Low-post defense requires defenders to aggressively deny the ball and get physical.

Your Can't-Miss Offensive Playbook

When you put five young, eager, and very inexperienced offensive players on the floor you're likely to see something like this: One player has the ball, and he dribbles and stops. Meanwhile, four other players jump up and down with arms in the air, calling out the name of the player with the ball: *Joey! Joey!* Translation: *Pass me the ball, Joey, so I can score!*

This is amusing to watch the first four or five times down the floor. It becomes less amusing each time afterward, until the coach's indulgent smile is replaced by a frown and then a crying jag. This is no way to run an offense, much less score a basket. From the defense's perspective, it's a gift. The chirping-bird offense is the easiest to shut down because it doesn't do much of anything except stand around. For a new player, the need to figure out what to do with the ball is apparent almost from the first practice. The ballhandler can dribble, pass, or shoot. The options are clear, even if the execution can take time to learn.

But there are five offensive players on the floor and only one ball to go around. What about the four would-be scoring machines who don't have the ball? One of the toughest things for new hoops hopefuls to learn is what to do when they're not dribbling, passing, or shooting. How do they contribute to the offense when they don't have the one essential ingredient for scoring a basket? Their first instinct is to find a way, any way, to get the ball. This usually involves various forms of pleading, jumping up and down, clapping hands, shouting names, offering bribes—whatever it takes to get a teammate to give up the ball and send it their way.

For the coach, understanding the mindset of his young sharpshooters isn't enough. The coach has to figure out how to make each player on the floor realize she has an important role to play in the offense, whether she has the ball or not. It's possible to turn five chirping birds into an offensive unit, but it takes time. Chances are, everything you practice will look like a mess the first few times it's tested under game conditions. The kids will inevitably forget everything and revert back to *Joey! Joey!* for a few quarters when pressured by a defense. They'll also find it hilarious when their long-suffering but ever-smiling coach imitates what they're doing during a time-out or at the next practice.

They'll laugh, but they'll get the message: Calling out each other's names and jumping up and down begging for a pass isn't any way to run an offense. Once they start scoring a few baskets off the simple but proven offenses explained in this chapter, *Joey! Joey!* will be a thing of the past. And once they master the basics of pass-cut-replace, they will have a foundation for just about any scoring scheme a coach can dream up, no matter how sophisticated.

Now, let's run some offense!

Applying Offensive Basics

No matter the specifics, all offenses share several big-picture traits. It's up to the coach to remind the players of these principles in practice and during games. Once the players grasp these ideas, it's only a matter of time before they turn into an unstoppable offensive force. (A coach can dream, right?)

- **Floor spacing.** Offensive players must maintain enough distance from each other that it will be difficult, if not impossible, for one defender to cover two people at once. Good spacing forces the defender to make a choice about which player to cover. Sometimes younger players will bunch together because it's difficult for them to pass the ball much more than 10 to 12 feet with accuracy and strength. But even these players will benefit if there is more space between defenders, because it will create more driving lanes to the basket. Please note that there are instances where offensive players must be close to each other—while setting a screen, for example. But for the most part, if you keep players from clinging together like a bunch of busy bees hovering around a honey jar, your offense will be better for it.

- **Player movement.** One of the hardest things for young players to learn is what to do on offense when they don't have the ball. Only one player has the basketball at any given time. So what do the other four players do, besides wave to their friends in the stands? They shouldn't stand around waiting for their turn with the ball. That's not how an efficient offense operates. They create! Players without the ball are the most important part of the offense, because they can create opportunities to score. They can set screens, cut to the basket, and work for rebounding position. They have a tremendous advantage because many defenders invariably focus on the player with the ball and lose sight of who they're guarding.

- **Ball movement.** Some kids don't like to share. Others are shy about asking for anything. The basketball court is a great place to break both habits. Teams that share the ball end up sharing a lot of victories. At the very least, they all feel like they're participating in the offense. As a general rule, emphasize less dribbling, more passing. *Swing the ball* is an appropriate mantra: Urge the players to pass the ball from one side of the court to the other and back again to keep the defense moving and to create seams between the defensive players for drives to the basket. Make sure that no one is frozen out. Certain players sometimes like to pass only to their friends or only to the better players on the team. A coach can't allow that to happen. Point out that missing or ignoring an open teammate isn't the way good basketball teams play the game. Players who share the ball should be showered with praise, back-slaps, and postgame pizza parties.

- **Patience.** Teams that race down the court and quickly put up shot after shot are doing the defense a big favor. Patience is not exactly a virtue shared by the young and the restless, but it's a concept that any good team must learn if it hopes to wear down an opponent. Sometimes the first shot is not the best shot. Sometimes, with a little work, a better shot materializes. Urge the players to keep the ball moving with safe passes and to work both sides of the court. Eventually, a scoring opportunity will open up and the team can take advantage. At the same time, a patient offense can wear out the opposing team—as opposed to wearing out their ever-patient coach. A patient offense can also pay off at the defensive end of the floor by helping a team catch its breath and re-energize for all-out defense while wearing out the other team.

- **Selflessness.** The best players are the best teammates—they make the rest of the team better with their selfless play on the court. This isn't accomplished by scoring all the points or dribbling the ball most of the time. This is a tough lesson to learn, but one that can be made by a coach who emphasizes that five players working together for a common goal can beat any single star player.

  Your players are not equal in talent; your job is to find each one's individual talent and emphasize it in a way that helps the entire team. Each player can discover how his talent can make the team—not the individual—shine. Sometimes that involves scoring a basket. Sometimes it means passing the ball or setting a screen to give a teammate the better opportunity. One way to emphasize this concept is to point to team accomplishments, not individual results: When a player is in the game, how is the team doing? Is it performing better or worse? If a player scores all her team's points but the team is still losing, what has been gained?

  Conversely, a player can make a huge positive difference in the outcome of a game without scoring a point. How? By making steals, completing smart passes to open teammates, diving on the floor for loose balls, playing tough defense, setting screens, and hustling up and down the floor. The teammate who cheers loudly on a rally, who always has a positive word for a player who just made a turnover, who looks to encourage and uplift no matter what the score, can make a difference just because of attitude. There are lots of ways to be a selfless teammate, and a coach should strive to build a roster full of them each season.

- **Communication.** Young players love to talk but not always at the most appropriate time. They usually decide to hold an intense conversation about what's on the next day's school lunch menu while the coach is giving an inspirational pregame speech. Conversely, when the game is in full swing, the magpies are suddenly mute. As with most things in basketball and in life, timing is everything. There's a time to talk and a time to listen.

  Players in the game need to communicate with each other verbally and physically. They should call plays, wave to a teammate to use a screen, or warn a fellow defender to avoid one. A player coming off a cut should send a signal with hands outstretched, communicating to the point guard where she wants a pass delivered. Players need to communicate with more than just their vocal cords. They need to see the whole court and see what each of their teammates is doing.

Encourage players to cut, move, and dribble with their heads up so they can communicate with their eyes. Make sure your players stash the lunch-menu conversations. There's plenty to talk about that applies to the game at hand.

- **Smarts.** Talent isn't everything. Hustle can compensate for a relative lack of physical ability. So can smarts. It's important to put players on the floor who know the plays, understand the game, and can carry out what the coach is asking them to do. If four players understand an offense but the fifth player on the floor does not, the offense will break down and points will come with greater difficulty. Encourage your players to keep their heads in the game and to watch and learn when they're sitting on the bench so they'll be prepared to play when they enter the game.

  Of course, we're talking about youngsters with infamously short attention spans. And some players can't tell the difference between being smart and being a smart aleck. A coach will undoubtedly encounter both behaviors on many teams. But kids also have the capacity to absorb a lot of new information in a short time. Tell them that smarts can make a big difference in the outcome of a game. Encourage them to ask questions if they don't understand something. Questions are the sign of an active mind—just the kind of mind any coach can appreciate.

You'll also want to use a numbering system to identify players in the offense. This makes it easier to draw up plays and gives players a better idea of where they should be positioned on the court relative to their teammates. Guards usually will be players 1 (point guard) and 2 (shooting guard). Forwards will be players 3 (small forward) and 4 (power forward). Centers will be player 5. These numbers move and interchange as your players move through an offense. Guards will find themselves down low. Forwards and centers will find themselves in the guard positions.

Playing the Pass-Cut-Replace

Pass-cut-replace is a basic building block of any offense and can be run against a man-to-man or zone defense. The principles underpinning it will apply to just about any other offense your team runs. It's also the simplest offense to learn, and it instantly involves five players. They'll all feel as if they're participating in the offense right away. It's hard to get bored when everyone's on the move.

Set up three players on the outside and two players on the inside, or *three out, two in*. This terminology can help the players visualize where they should be on the floor and make them aware of floor spacing. There should always be a point guard and two wings (players 1, 2, and 3) on the outside and two forwards (players 4 and 5) on the low post (see figure 5.1). Start practicing the offense with players 1, 2, and 3 at first, then add players 4 and 5 later.

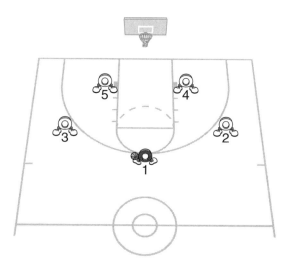

Figure 5.1   Three-out, two-in offensive set.

To run the offense, the point (1) makes an entry pass to either wing (2) and then cuts toward the basket off the elbow closest to the wing with the ball (figure 5.2). The wing player (3) on the opposite side replaces the point at the top of the key. In moving to the point guard position, the wing should shake off any defenders by cutting toward the basket first (V-cut), then out to the top of the key. The first cutter (1) moves through the lane ready to receive a return pass. After clearing the lane, the cutter moves to the opposite wing to restore the "three-out" alignment.

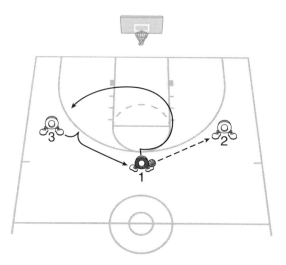

Figure 5.2   Guard movement for entry pass.

The offense can also begin by dribbling the ball from the point to the wing (figure 5.3). This calls for a *shallow cut*. This enables the best ballhandler, the point guard (1), to remain in control of the ball. The wing player (2) and the point guard (1) trade positions, with the wing player taking a few steps over the top of the defender toward the basket and then cutting back to the point. This leaves the wing position open for the dribble entry. It also creates move-

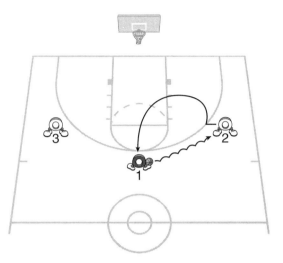

Figure 5.3 Guard movement when point dribbles to wing and wing makes a shallow cut.

ment away from the ball and ensures proper floor spacing.

Once the team understands the three-guard rotation, add the low-post players (4 and 5), who line up on opposite low blocks. When the ball is passed from point (1) to wing (2), the low-post player (4) on the ball side moves to the ball-side corner (figure 5.4). As before, after making the pass, the point cuts through the lane on the basketball side and looks for the pass on the give-and-go, and the opposite wing moves to the point. If the pass is not thrown, the point (1) rotates to the weak-side wing. The weak-side wing (3) replaces 1 at point position.

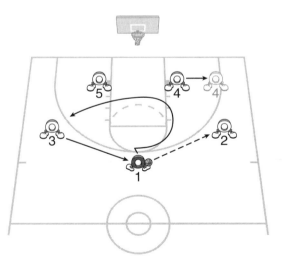

Figure 5.4 Guard and forward movement on pass to the wing.

The wing (2) passes the ball to the corner (4), then the wing (2) cuts to the basket and out to the opposite wing (figure 5.5), replacing 1 who moves back to the point. The players on the outside are constantly passing, cutting, and "replacing" one another on the perimeter, so the offense can run continuously for as long as required to get off a shot. A pass back to the point is used only to rotate the ball to the opposite side of the floor and, as a result, does not involve any basket cuts or rotation.

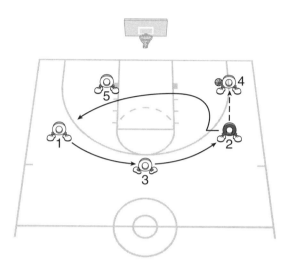

Figure 5.5 After passing to the corner, the wing cuts to the basket.

When the ball has been passed to the wing, the strong-side forward (4) rotates to the strong-side corner as already noted. This movement allows the lane to clear for all basket cutters. After the wing (2) rotates through to the weak-side wing, the weak-side low-post player (5) flashes the lane, moving from the low block to midlane or the help line (figure 5.6). This must be a quick movement to avoid violating the three-second rule. As discussed previously, the ball can be passed down to 4 in the strong-side corner, which allows for another basket cut (give-and-go) by the wing guard (3).

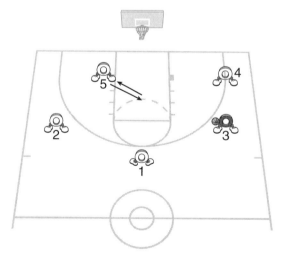

Figure 5.6 Weak-side forward flashes lane for a potential pass.

Coaching Points

Players should always rotate to maintain the three-out, two-in setup. Make sure players spread out the defense with proper spacing; there should be about 10 to 12 feet between each offensive player. When in doubt, basket cut. The player with the ball should cut to the basket after passing to a wing or corner.

Attacking a Zone Defense

Teams play zone defenses to keep defenders close to the basket and cut down on layups. Teams may also play zone because it's easier to teach than man-to-man defense because players cover an area rather than chasing another player. Zone defenses enable teams to hide players who are slower or do not play man-to-man defense well. A zone is especially effective against offenses that rely on one or two strong players to attack the basket. Zone defenses can close off opportunities to offensive players who want to dribble and drive to the basket. This can frustrate a young team and compel them to heave brick after brick at the basket from far outside their shooting range. Not a pretty sight. To prevent a massive migraine and an 0-for-78 shooting night by her team, a coach needs to keep herself and her team calm, and emphasize three key strategies for beating a zone.

1. **Be patient.** Against zone defenses, impatience can lead an offense to heave up shots that will make a coach turn three shades of red. Most kids can't wait for anything, let alone something as much fun as taking a shot in a basketball game, so teaching patience against a zone will require a lot of practice . . . and patience. But the players need to learn that it will take several passes and several ball rotations each time down the floor before a good shot presents itself against a tightly packed zone. Remember, there is no shot clock in youth basketball, so there's no limit on how long a team can work the ball.

   You can help the offense get in the proper mindset by offering timely reminders: *Slow down*, *Patience*, and the old reliable, *What's the hurry?* Unless time is running out in a close game and the team desperately needs a basket to catch up, players need to recognize that running an offense is not a race. This is something that should be worked on in practice; it will help the players realize that passing the ball and working patiently for a shot is what smart offenses must do to break down a zone defense.

2. **Attack the "gray areas."** The gaps between defensive players can widen when the zone defense moves, and these represent where the defense is most vulnerable. Offensive players should step into gray areas to receive a pass or shoot the basketball. They can also drive to the basket by cutting through the gray areas. When that happens, two defensive players sometimes collapse to stop the penetration, which allows for a pass to an open offensive player.

3. **Keep moving the ball.** Zone defenses are effective against teams that do not use both sides of the floor. Teach your team to reverse the ball from one side of the floor to the other several times to spread out the zone. The more your team rotates the ball back and forth, the larger the gray areas will become as the defense stretches out. In practice, have the kids work on passing the ball at least three times each possession.

To accomplish these strategies for attacking a zone, the offensive team should create a staggered front, depending on how many defenders are up top.

Attacking With a Three-Guard Set

If the defense is set up with two players up top in a 2-1-2 or 2-3 zone, attack with a three-guard set: one point guard (1) and two wings (player 2 on the right and player 4 on the left), as shown in figure 5.7. Player 5 will be in the low post on the same side as 2. Player 3 will be in the opposite corner on the same side as 4.

The point guard (1) does not cut toward the basket, but keeps moving in the area across the top of the key so he can pass the ball to the wings and rotate the ball to the opposite side of the court. The two wings and the forward and center work together to create movement and scoring opportunities. As shown in figure 5.8, player 1 will pass to 4 on the wing, 4 will pass down to 3 in the corner, and 4 will cut toward the basket through

Figure 5.7   Setup for attacking with a three-guard offensive set.

the lane and rotate out to the weak-side wing. After 4 has cut through, 5 and 2 will cut toward the ball in search of gray-area weak spots in the zone. Their hands should be outstretched, ready to receive a pass from 3. Player 2 proceeds through the free-throw line area and continues to the opposite wing, which 4 has vacated. Player 5 flashes the lane and looks for a pass while moving from the low block to the opposite low block. Player 1 moves to an open

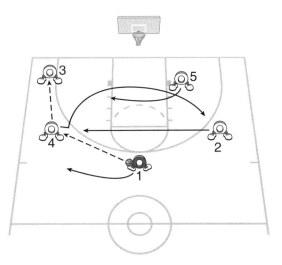

Figure 5.8 Player movement for the three-guard attack.

spot on the strong side of the floor above the free-throw line in case 3 is pressured and can't find an open cutter. Once the weak-side wing cuts across to the strong side, 1 moves back to the point.

The idea is to attack from the weak side; the weak-side cutters can take advantage of the defenders' attention to the ball side and find gaps in the zone, where they can receive passes and convert them into scores. The weak-side elbow at the free-throw line can be particularly vulnerable and presents a scoring opportunity for the weak-side wing on a skip pass. If the cutters are not open, quick ball rotation can create an open shot for the corner player (3). After passing the ball to a post player, wing, or point guard, 3 should run the baseline to the opposite corner while the rest of the team rotates the ball to 3's side of the court.

This scheme plays out in following manner. After 3 passes to one of the cutters from the weak side (2 or 5), 3 runs the baseline to the opposite corner, on the same side as 4 (figure 5.9). The player who receives the pass from 3 (usually 2)

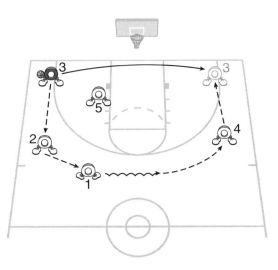

Figure 5.9 Weak-side attack by reversing the ball.

passes to 1, and 1 looks to reverse the ball quickly to 4, who sends it to player 3. If a shot does not result, the ofense begins again.

Attacking With a Two-Guard Set

If the defense is in a 1-3-1 or 1-2-2 zone, attack with a two-guard front (1 and 2), two post players (4 and 5), and a "runner" (3) on the baseline as shown in figure 5.10. Players 1 and 5 line up on the same side, 2 and 4 on the opposite side. Player 3 should line up in the strong-side corner.

Player 1 initiates by looking to 3 in the corner, 5 in the low post, or 4 flashing from the weak-side low post to the strong-side elbow. If player 3 receives the pass (figure 5.11), 3 looks to pass to 5 in the low post or to 4 flashing to the elbow. The strong-side low-post player (5) can screen to create an open shot for 3. Player 1 stays above the free-throw line and looks for a return pass from 3 or a pass from 4 or 5 if player 3 has passed to one of them. After 3 passes the ball to player 5, 4, or 1, player 3 runs the baseline to the opposite corner (figure 5.12). When 1 gets the ball back (see figure 5.13), she can then pass the ball to 2 on the opposite side of the court (this is called a *ball reversal* because it changes the strong side of the court). Then 2 looks to pass to the baseline runner (3) moving toward the strong-side corner for a shot, while 4 flashes from the elbow to the strong-side low post, and 5 flashes from the low post to the strong-side elbow. Then the offense starts again.

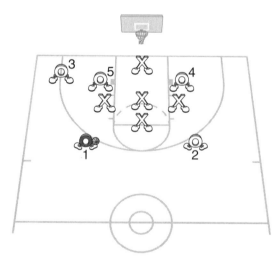

Figure 5.10 Offensive attack with a two-guard front and a baseline runner.

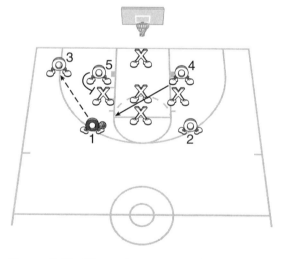

Figure 5.11 Player 1 passes to player 3 in the corner. Player 5 may screen and player 4 flashes from low post to the elbow.

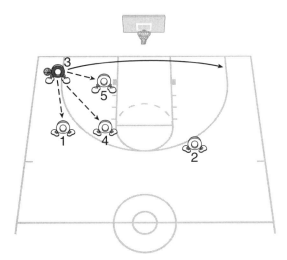

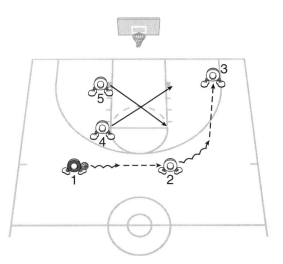

Figure 5.12 Player 3 passes and cuts across base line to opposite corner.

Figure 5.13 Player 1 reverses the ball while 5 flashes from the low post to the elbow and 4 flashes from the elbow to the low post.

Coaching Points

When attacking a zone defense, the point guard needs to stay above the free-throw line and keep active, bouncing from one side of the floor to the other. More than any other player on the floor, the point guard's job is to ensure that the offense keeps swinging the ball back and forth and uses both sides of the floor. The offense will stall if it operates on only one side of the floor.

Players should look to find cutters and make quick passes to them when possible. Passers should always look to the low post as the first option because it's closest to the basket. Cutters should avoid simply running to an assigned spot on the floor; they should have their hands out and be ready to receive a quick pass in a gray area between defenders anywhere en route to their destination.

Players should keep the ball moving with crisp passes. They should reverse the ball to stretch out the defense and make the defenders work. Against defenders who focus on the strong side and turn their backs to the weak side, players should attack the weak side with basket cuts and ball reversals. The dribble should be used to attack the defensive gaps. If the defense collapses, the ballhandler should pass to open teammates on the outside. If the defense is slow to react, the ballhandler should drive to the basket.

The offense against a zone provides multiple options for passers and cutters. But the players should be encouraged to improvise. A coach doesn't want robots running the same predictable sequences over and over again. Players should not lose sight of the basic object of the game: put the ball in the basket. They should be looking for openings and scoring opportunities, and as they become comfortable with the offense they should be encouraged to ad-lib. This is guaranteed to look like a mess at first, but over time the players will begin to move with greater purpose, and an effective offense will begin to take shape.

Attacking a Man-to-Man Defense

The strategy against a man-to-man must be different than against a zone. Against a man-to-man defense, offensive players will face an up-tempo, aggressive, pressure defense—at least some of the time. Scoring opportunities will be more frequent than against a zone, and so will opportunities for mistakes. The pace of the game will accelerate, leading to more scoring, more missed shots, more turnovers, more fast breaks, and more mayhem. But the offense can't get caught up in the frenzy. It needs to take advantage of it.

Spacing and player movement, again, will be crucial to the offensive team's success; however, offenses that are effective against man-to-man defenses also incorporate the element of screening. Cutting in front of (top side) rather than behind the defender to get open will be key to the success of these offenses. The top-side cut ensures that there will be a clear passing line between the passer and the cutter.

Four Out, One In

Against any defense, the offense should try to spread the floor—create wide gaps between defenders—and that's especially true against man-to-man. But as a coach you can only space your players as far as they can throw the ball. It's pointless to put 12 to 15 feet between your offensive players if one or two of them can throw the ball that far only with a four-step wind-up. It might look impressive in practice, but in the game it'll get whistled for traveling every time. So adjust and improvise.

Urge your players to spread out the defense but to cut down the distance between passer and receiver by having the receivers step to every pass. A passer can't take four steps to heave a ball, but a receiver can take four steps toward the ball in preparing to catch it. This will still encourage ball and player movement, and it won't cost the team a turnover or short-circuit the coach's already fragile nervous system.

The other potential pitfall of this offense is poor or nonexistent cutting by the offensive players. This marks the dreaded return of the chirping-bird offense. *I'm open, I'm open,* Alyssa yells, while a defender stands no more than two feet away, ready to intercept a pass. Alyssa needs to V-cut to get open: move toward the basket to force the defender to back up, and then move back to the original position to receive a pass. Timing is key. Encourage your pass receivers to create a target for the passer while cutting back to their original position, and encourage the passers to pass the ball as the receiver is coming out of his cut, not when he completes the cut and is once again a stationary target. Chirp, chirp.

With those basics in place, the four-out, one-in offense can be very effective. It is a simple, one-screen offense. It can be used as a stall-type offense to run clock or as a regular offensive set.

Four players arrange themselves in box-shaped formation (see figure 5.14). On one side, player 1 is the wing and player 3 is in the corner. On the opposite side, player 2 is on the wing and player 4 is in the corner. Player 5 is "in" above the free-throw line, close to the three-point line. Player 5 is the primary screener; the other four players will rotate in either a clockwise or counterclockwise rotation. The offense starts with 1 on the

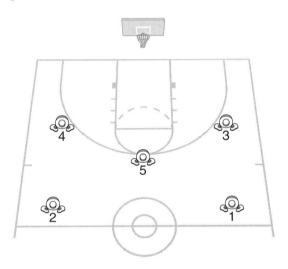

Figure 5.14   Four-out, one-in offensive setup.

wing, who passes to 3 in the corner and cuts to the basket on the ball side. Player 2 cuts from the opposite wing toward 5 above the free-throw line, and has three options as 5 sets a screen, depending on how the defender reacts to the screen:

1. Cut out to the opposite wing (if the defender drops into the lane area behind the screen) as shown in figure 5.15. (Player 4 cuts to the wing to replace 2, and 1 replaces 4 in the corner; 3 passes to 1 as 1 cuts or to 2 on the wing.)

2. Curl around the screen toward the basket (if the defender runs into the screen) as shown in figure 5.16.

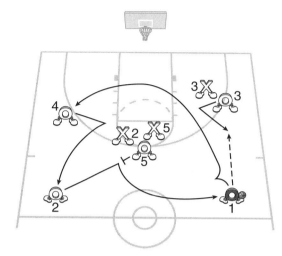

Figure 5.15   Option 1: Player 2 cuts out to wing.   **Figure 5.16**   Option 2: Player 2 curls to basket.

3. Cut behind the screen (back-door cut) toward the basket (if the defender tries to run above or over the top of the screen) as shown in figure 5.17.

To simplify, use option 1 exclusively at first, to get the players used to the idea of where and how to move. Once the players get comfortable with the basic pattern of the offense, then encourage them to look to score by adding options 2 and 3.

Emphasize that this offense is designed to create scoring

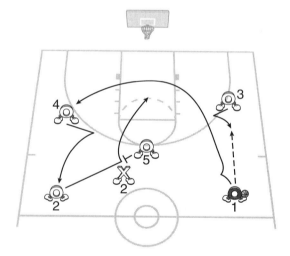

Figure 5.17   Option 3: Player 2 makes a back-door cut to the basket.

opportunities early in the game. By spreading the floor, the four out, one in offense can create a lot of gaps in the defense. After catching a pass, each player should square up to the basket and look to drive for a layup against a single defender before continuing the offense with another pass. Avoid logjams in the lane: only one player at a time should cut to the basket

As the players learn the offense, try to get them to run the offense from both sides of the floor so they don't become so predictable. Rotation of the four outside players can be clockwise or counterclockwise. To reverse the ball to the opposite side of the floor (see figure 5.18), the strong-side wing (1) should take a couple of dribbles toward the opposite wing (2) to avoid a long crosscourt pass and then pass as sharply as

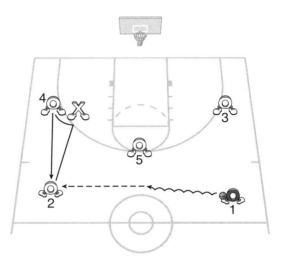

Figure 5.18 Reversing the ball to rotate outside players in the opposite direction.

possible to 2. If 2 is closely covered by a defender and can't get open for the pass, 2 can move toward the weak-side corner (4) and set a screen on the corner defender, then 4 moves up to the weak-side wing position to receive a pass from 1, and the offense begins again.

Coaching Points

The strong-side corner must V-cut toward the basket above the defender and then cut back to the corner to receive a pass from the wing. If the defender overplays the strong-side corner, the strong-side corner can cut to the basket and receive a pass from the strong-side wing (back-door cut). The weak-side wing must run toward the free-throw-line area and shake off the defender against the screen; the wing then cuts sharply at a 45-degree angle out to the opposite wing.

Players should maintain floor spacing. After cutting off a screen at the free-throw line, a wing should be at least 8 feet away from a screener before receiving a pass from the strong-side corner. The cutter should receive the ball on the way to the wing, not when the cutter arrives at the wing and is stationary. This prevents defenders from clustering around the ball and makes the pass more difficult to intercept.

Timing is everything. Good timing and proper floor spacing allows the offense to run smoothly and prevents cutters from becoming entangled on the way to the basket.

One Out, Four In

The one-out, four-in (or *fire*) offensive play is designed to create a quick scoring opportunity. This is not an offense that should be run more than once or twice a game, as it is designed for one player. But it can be an effective change of pace. Coaches should avoid singling out one or two players to always run this particular offense; make sure each player on the team has an opportunity to experience what it feels

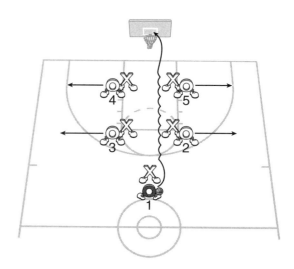

Figure 5.19 One-out, four-in (fire) offensive play.

like to run fire over the course of a few games. For players who don't normally get the ball in a one-on-one situation, it can be a marvelous way to promote aggressiveness and driving to the basket.

The offense starts with one player (1) with the ball on top, two players (4 and 5) opposite each other on the low blocks, and two players (2 and 3) opposite each other at the elbows (figure 5.19). Player 1 calls *Fire!* and the offensive players head to the sidelines as far away from the basket as possible in an attempt to draw away their defenders and leave the lane unprotected: 4 and 5 move toward opposite corners, and 2 and 3 move out toward opposite sidelines (free-throw line extended). This gives 1 an opportunity to take on a defender one-on-one and score.

This can be an opportunity for some individual creativity. Coaches should encourage 1 to use the space to attack the basket with something other than a straight-ahead dribble with the strong hand. Instead, use it as an opportunity to try out a crossover dribble, and aim to get a shot off in the lane (preferably a layup) rather than settle for an outside shot. If 1 is stopped short of the basket or runs into difficulty, there are several options (figure 5.20):

1. If one or more help defenders collapse into the lane to prevent the drive, 1 can pass the ball to the offensive player left open on the wing or in the corner for an outside shot.

2. The corner players closest to the basket can cut into the lane and look to receive a pass from 1.

3. One of the wings can cut up to the point position (shallow cut) to receive a pass from 1 and reset the offense.

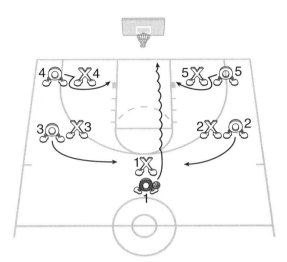

Figure 5.20   If player 1 runs into difficulty, reset the offense.

Managing Breakdowns and Transitions

Every offense, no matter how good, breaks down or gets out of sync. But at the youth basketball level, this isn't an exception—it's the norm. How the players manage this state of nearly perpetual chaos will be an ongoing test for any offense, and for any coach's digestion. Just keep telling yourself *It's only a game* and your stomach should settle, even if the offense doesn't.

Kids are more accustomed to chaos, anyway, and if your offense is in disarray, just imagine what the defense (and the opposing coach) is going through. At this point, the worst thing a coach can do is start barking instructions that involve more than one or two syllables. It will only add to the sense of disarray. Chances are, everybody in the stands will be offering well-intentioned but barely intelligible advice, too. And the players on the floor also will be doing their share of yelling as they try to unscramble the circuits between their ears. So what you have is a gym that sounds like an auto factory in full scream. It's impossible to prepare your team for these moments, but once they happen during a game, they can turn into a teaching tool: *Remember when three of the five players on the floor forgot to run the offense? How can we handle that situation in the future?*

Tell your players that the best thing to do is to start the offense over from the beginning. Because there's usually not a shot clock to worry about, your team needs to recognize that they have time to reset. There's no reason to hurry, and no pressure to get off a shot (unless it's the very last minute of the game, of course, and you're behind by only a basket or two).

It'd be nice if one with-it player on the floor took charge, but it's likely that even the most talented players will be too caught up in the confusion to think about the needs of the whole team. So it may be up to you to briefly break your vow of silence and contribute one loud but simple command: Reset! This will signal the rest of the team to return to their original positions and try again.

Sometimes it may take several tries before a team gets in sync again, but usually when a couple of kids on the floor suddenly get it, the others can at least fake it. Remember, unless the other team is composed of future pro-basketball stars, the chaos should cut both ways. It may take several weeks and much trial and error in games for a team to run their plays correctly in the heat of competition. Don't be frustrated if the team runs an offense relatively well in practice, and then forgets all about it once they start keeping score. During time-outs or halftime, a coach can redraw the play on the dry-erase board and refresh everyone's memory.

If all else fails, another simple command can at least get the players to look like they know what they're doing: *Pass and cut*. Rather than dribbling the ball willy-nilly or standing around the perimeter looking lost, the players will at least remember that basketball is a team sport requiring ball movement and player movement. If a coach can see those two things happening on the floor during a basketball game, life is good, no matter what offense your team thinks it's running.

Also, any offense should always be prepared to transition to defense. The key to this is always having at least one player at the point, above the free-throw arc, to prevent the other team from rebounding a missed shot and quickly scoring a fast-break layup at an undefended basket. That is why it's important for the players to rotate properly. If each of these offensive sets is run correctly, there will always be an offensive player at the point position, ready to sprint back on defense.

That's right, *sprint*. Get your team in the habit of hustling back on defense as fast as their legs can move them. This gets them in position sooner to defend the basket, and ensures that they will beat the ball up the court. The easiest way to score in youth basketball is the uncontested layup off a 1-on-0 or 2-on-0 fast break, where the offensive team doesn't have to beat a single defender. Just one defender hustling back on defense can prevent this from happening and instantly give your team a better chance of winning the game, or at least staying close.

Players who transition back on defense should get in the habit of running hard at the basket they are defending until they reach half-court, where they should turn around to the open defensive position (back turned to basket being defended, knees slightly bent, arms wide). The defender's job at this point is twofold:

1. Stay ahead of any offensive players running toward the basket.
2. Stop, or at least slow down, the advance of the ball by staying ahead of the ballhandler and giving the defender's teammates time to catch up.

The Coach's Clipboard

✔ Spread the floor and force the defense to make a choice about which player to cover.

✔ Players without the ball should cut to the basket, set screens, and work for rebound position.

✔ *Less dribbling, more passing is the key to good ball movement.*

✔ Patience leads to good shots.

✔ Pass first, shoot second.

✔ Communication—verbal and physical—underscores teamwork.

✔ Pass-cut-replace is a go-to offense against any defense.

✔ Ball movement and patience can break down a zone defense.

✔ Four-out, one-in offense will spread the floor against man-to-man.

✔ Reset the offense if a play breaks down.

Surefire Defensive Sets

Individual defense is about desire. Desire comes naturally to any kid who loves to play basketball. But team defense means combining desire with smarts, and smarts have to be nurtured. This will take time, patience, and several bottles of aspirin.

Defense is all about effort, all the time. It means no defender can afford to be an observer, even if his man no longer has the ball and the basket is being attacked on the opposite side of the floor. Just like a well-oiled offense, a defense must move together and share responsibility for stopping any offensive threat. This can be a tough lesson to learn. From a young player's perspective, the rewards for stopping a score aren't nearly as immediate and gratifying as scoring yourself. A coach can change that mindset by emphasizing and rewarding defensive stops.

But first, a reality check. Realize that during the first few practices it's likely that nobody on the team will know what a 2-3 zone is or who they're supposed to be covering in a man-to-man. It may even take a few games before the players know when they are on defense or offense, or which direction they are going with the ball. Don't be surprised if one of your players gets a steal on defense and goes the wrong way to score a basket for the other team. When that happens, there is only one possible response: Applaud and say, *Great hustle!* So stifle that scream, Coach. A steal is a steal, and that kind of effort will eventually lead to great defense.

Building a Defense

You'll need to take baby steps at first when teaching your team to play defense. Discourage your defenders from clustering around the ball. Try not to let them get stretched too far away from the basket. You always want to have at least one or two defenders in the free-throw lane—at the help line—to prevent easy baskets and layups. (The help line is an imaginary line that splits the court in half horizontally from basket to basket.) And you want your defenders playing with their backs to the basket they're defending, sliding to the strong side (ball side), rather than turning their backs on either their assigned player or the ball. If those basics sink in over a team's first season, you and your team will have accomplished a lot. It also will mean constant gentle reminders from you, the ever-patient coach, to your players in the heat of a game: *Help line! Open up! See your man, see the ball!*

Team defense, like an offense, is achieved slowly, over a season. It's one of the first steps toward building a true team, but it's a giant step. So, again, be patient. Look for tiny flashes of improvement rather than consistent, lockdown defense over an entire game. It won't happen. And if, by some miracle, it does happen, do a handstand—or at least clap real loud to let your players know they've done something special.

Start with a zone defense; it's appropriate for any age group, and players can learn it quickly. In a zone, defenders cover a particular area on the court. And believe it or not, it's easier for beginners to grasp covering an area rather than covering another player man-to-man. That's because a man-to-man defense requires the defender to guard an offensive player all over the floor yet see the basketball at all times. That's a tough concept to learn, let alone put into practice, even for an experienced defender. You'll see a lot of young defenders chasing their man willy-nilly all over the floor, while opponents are driving to the basket and scoring at will behind them. It's part of the (very steep) learning curve, and it's the kind of stuff that can drive even the most even-keeled coach nuts. But read on, Coach. There's hope—and better defense—ahead.

Given the challenges of man-to-man defense, the beginner coach with the beginner team might seem to have an easy choice: Just play zone all the time. Don't make that mistake. Playing and understanding man-to-man defense will improve a player's zone defense, so it's important to learn both. Work on man-to-man a little bit at every practice, and vow to play it for at least half a game every game once the season gets rolling, even if a few of your players give up easy baskets. Remember, even NBA stars get burned playing one-on-one. The key is to get your players thinking like a team on defense. Once they do, scoring will become tougher for your opponents, and defense will become a strength of your team.

In most younger leagues, full-court pressing is not allowed, so as to give the players an opportunity to learn how the game works. This is a gift from the heavens. A full-court press can pick up the speed and energy of a game but also increase the level of chaos and the atmosphere of panic. It's difficult for young players to learn how to play the game properly when they're either pressing the other team or being pressed all the time. In any case, it's imperative that a young team learn how to play half-court defense before moving on to a press, and half-court defense will be the focus of this chapter.

2-1-2 Zone Defense

The zone defense is a great way to slow down an offense and force a team into a more patient style. Patience—now there's a word you don't often hear associated with youth-league offenses. Zone defenders should use that to their advantage. Teams that try to bust into a 2-1-2 zone (see figure 6.1) with dribble drives see that penetration to the basket is more difficult because the lanes to the basket are closed off. As a result, most teams will settle for outside shots, which are not a strength of most youth-league players.

A zone can cover up individual deficiencies on defense. It can hide weaker players and protect slower defenders from getting burned by great ballhandlers. But for a zone to be effective, players must realize that just because they cover an area doesn't mean it's nap time when the ball's on the other side of the court. A zone is not code for "zoning out." Players need to be just as alert, assertive, and ball-conscious as when they are playing man-to-man.

Most beginner players see a zone as an opportunity to settle into a particular spot on the floor and stay there. But good zone defense is built on quick, controlled movement. Players have an assigned area, and their position within that area will change each time the ball moves. With each pass by the offense, all five defenders on the zone must adjust their floor position. They need to jump to the ball as a team, or else they risk

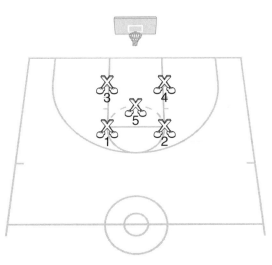

Figure 6.1 Setup for 2-1-2 zone defense.

creating lanes for the offense to exploit. As with man-to-man defense, the defenders must work together and help each other close off scoring opportunities.

The two guards at the top of the zone must cover point and wings. One guard will play the ball as the ball moves into the frontcourt. It doesn't matter which guard does this, but the two guards must communicate. A simple verbal signal (*I got her!*) may be all that's needed at first, and eventually the defenders will begin to react instinctively with the guard closest to the ballhandler moving out to defend.

As shown in figure 6.2, guards should not move beyond the three-point arc to cover the point guard (1). If they go beyond the arc, they won't have time to drop down and cover the wing (2). The other guard should be positioned at about the elbow. From this position, the guard can move out and cover the wing (3) on his side after 3 receives a pass. The guard is also in position to cut off any offensive cutters through the lane. If the point guard passes to the opposite wing (2), the point defender must drop to cover 2 (see figure 6.3), and the wing defender must drop to just below the free-throw line to cut off any drives and be prepared to jump out and cover 1.

Forwards must "show" to the wing if 2 or 3 receives a pass and is momentarily left uncovered by one of the guards. On a pass to 2 or 3, forwards must advance several steps toward the wing. They should not close out or cover 2 or 3. The purpose of this "show" maneuver is to make

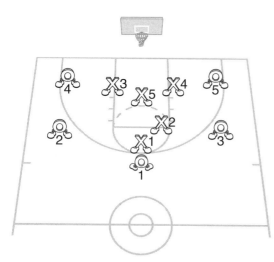

Figure 6.2 In zone defense, one guard covers point and both stay below the three-point line.

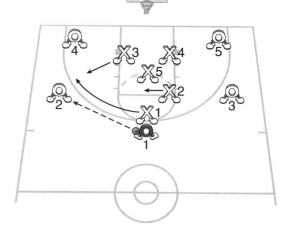

Figure 6.3 On a pass to the wing, the point defender moves to cover the wing. The other guard moves to the help line and the strong-side forward shows to the wing.

2 or 3 pause and give the guard time to recover and defend 2 or 3.

The defensive center must step up in the middle of the lane and cut off any drives to the basket or block any offensive players with an arm bar as they flash the lane looking for a quick pass and a close-in shot. When the strong-side forward moves to show to the wings or defend the corner (figure 6.4), the center must move into the vacated low-block position and cut off entry passes to the low post. The

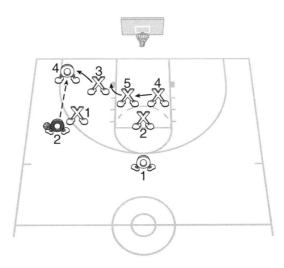

Figure 6.4 On a pass to the corner, the forward closes out the corner, the center moves to the low block, and the weak-side forward moves to the center.

weak-side forward will shift to the middle position vacated by the center. Forwards must close out the corner player (4) on their side of the floor when the corner receives a pass.

Coaching Points

Defenders must jump to the strong side and move while the ball is in the air on the pass. They should stay open to the ball and the weak side. Forwards who show to the wing must not leave the wing until called off by the guard who is recovering from the point. The weak-side guard should drop just under the free-throw line to cut off any cutters through the lane and cover the point on a pass back to the point.

Man-to-Man Defense

Man-to-man defense is a foundation of any great defensive team. This defense might also be called the *help defense*, because no defender is an island in man-to-man. It's everyone's responsibility to stop the ball and prevent the easy basket, but this needs to be done in coordinated fashion. All man-to-man defenders need to understand that they have a role to play no matter where the ball is on the court and that their roles will change every time the ball is passed.

One of the most difficult things for new defenders to learn is that they shouldn't all be running after the player with the ball. The second hardest thing to learn is that even when they're playing man-to-man, they should not just exclusively cover their assigned offensive player. They need to be aware of where the ball is on the court at all times, even when their player doesn't have the ball. And they need to help stop the ball, even if the offensive player doing the ballhandling isn't their assigned player.

Coaching Points

Since beginners sometimes struggle to remember which player they're supposed to guard, some leagues use colored wrist bands to pair up defensive and offensive players. Each offensive player wears a different color wristband. Then each defensive player wears a wristband of the same color as the offensive player he should be guarding.

Defenders who are more than one pass away should move to an open stance at the help line. This will enable them to see both their assigned player on the weak side and the ball on the strong side and will put them in position to protect the basket against drives and layups. Help-line defense is guaranteed to befuddle even your smartest players at first. The natural tendency is for defenders to follow their assigned offensive player anywhere on the court. But if they abandon the help line to follow their man, the defense breaks down, which leads to the Red Sea effect: a parting of the sea of defenders that leaves the lane wide open for easy baskets.

Help line! will become the coach's battle cry. With each game, it'll sound less desperate and be less necessary as your kids become familiar with the concept. The key is to get the defensive team to realize that each time the ball position changes, all defenders must also change position in relation to their assigned player, the ball, and the basket they are defending.

Another one of the central commandments of man-to-man is *below the man, below the ball.* A defender should always be in position to help teammates defend the basket. If the ball is 15 feet away from the basket, but a strong-side help defender is 20 feet away from the basket, that means the defender is "above" the ball and in poor position to help the ball defender.

It takes time for young players to learn these concepts, so be prepared for well-meaning mistakes and outright confusion. But mistakes and confusion create opportunities for a coach to teach. And though man-to-man implies a certain amount of individuality, it actually nurtures broader team concepts. There is nothing more selfless and team oriented than playing help defense.

The best way to teach your team man-to-man defense is to walk through it under simulated game conditions in practice, five against five. (The shell drill on page 99, in which four defenders shift position on the floor in relation to the ball, can give you a head start on these concepts.) Set up your players by placing five offensive players around the perimeter: one player on the point (1), two wing players (2 and 3), and two corner players (4 and 5). Then, add five defenders to match up with each offensive player.

During the walk-through, the focus should be for each of the defenders to achieve the proper position and stance each time the ball moves. As the ball is passed around the perimeter, offensive players should hold the basketball for a two count to let the defense move and the coaches see how each defensive player is adjusting. Defenders should not try to intercept passes or make steals.

If the ball is on the point (1) as shown in figure 6.5, the point defensive player is in defensive stance and closes out, the wing players (defending 2 and 3) must be in a deny stance, and the two corner defensive players (4 and 5) will be in an open stance at the help line. If the ball is on the wing (2) as shown in figure 6.6, the strong-side wing player closes out, the corner player on the strong side will deny the first pass away to 4, the point player will deny the first pass away to 1, and the weak-side wing and corner will slide over to the help line while staying open to 3 and 5. If the

Figure 6.5 Setup for man-to-man defense.

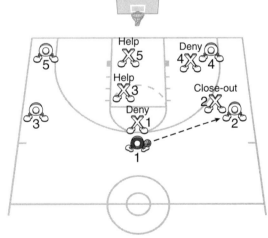

Figure 6.6 On a pass to the wing, defenders must adjust their defensive stance based on the new location of the ball.

ball is in the corner with 4 as shown in figure 6.7, the corner defender closes out on 4, the strong-side wing denies the first pass away to 2, the point will fall to just below the free-throw line in an open stance, and the weak-side wing and corner will be at the help line while staying open to 3 and 5.

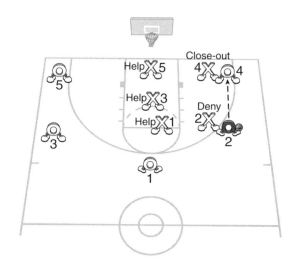

Figure 6.7   On a pass to the corner, the defenders must adjust to the new location of the ball.

Offenses will use screens against man-to-man sets, and defenders must be prepared for them. Defenders facing screens have two options: Get through or around the screen, or switch offensive players. At the younger age levels, switching should not bring about too many mismatches. But as players grow and size mismatches become an issue, or if offensive players have developed a great outside shot, you might not want to switch in your defensive matchups.

For now, encourage the players to get through screens and stick with their assigned offensive player. This will require communication. Defenders who cover screeners must alert their teammates that a screen is being set with a loud warning: *Screen left, Kelly!* That way the defender has time to see or feel the screen and work around it. In addition, the defender who has shouted the warning needs to help her teammate by *hedging*, a movement in which the defender drops a few feet closer to the basket to cut off the driving lane for the ballhandler while still keeping her man in sight (see figures 6.8 *a* and *b*). Hedging also creates a few feet of space for the defender's teammate to catch up with the ballhandler. Then regular defensive positioning can resume (this is called *help and recovery*).

Defenders need to communicate to team up against screens, and communication is a key element to great defense in general. It should be an easy lesson to impart, one would assume, because kids love to talk. They'll yak during practice, they'll yap on the bench, they'll chirp while the coach is talking. But put them in a game, and suddenly they press the mute button. Encourage your players to communicate on the court. Make sure substitutes understand they need to talk with the player they are replacing, so they know who they are supposed to be guarding when

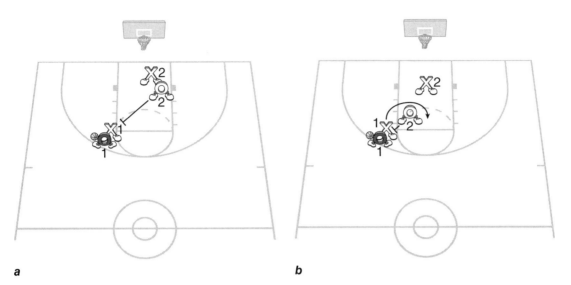

Figure 6.8 (*a*) Offensive player 2 setting a screen for offensive player 1. (*b*) The defender covering player 2 hedges and moves only part way up the lane, cutting off a potential drive and allowing space for the other defender to move around the screen.

they enter the game. Additionally, when the other team sends in subs, new matchups must be made accordingly.

This may seem like a lot for players to absorb, but they'll figure it out sooner if they talk. If they don't talk, they're even more confused, and they lose. Getting kids to ask each other *Who do you have?* is one of the first and quickest ways to establish that verbal communication is a key part to playing great defense.

During a game, each coach should have a mental checklist of questions that each player needs to be able to answer. In time, the coach won't need to ask these questions, because his hard-working defenders will have answered them already. But early in the season, each player should expect to hear the following questions from his coach:

- **Who are you covering?** Each player should know the number of the person she is assigned to defend.

- **Why are you chasing your player?** Novice man-to-man defenders usually need to be reminded several times a game that they need to stay in front of the offensive player to block his path to basket. If they chase, they'll have a great view of each layup scored against them.

- **Why are you covering the tallest player when you are one of the shorter players?** Players should learn to match up according to size. Sometimes a small player will replace a taller player. They should learn to switch defensive assignments with one of their teammates on the floor.

- **Where is the help defense?** Defenders need to avoid the Red Sea effect, and have at least one or two weak-side defenders in the lane at all times to discourage easy baskets and drives through the lane.

- **Why is the other team scoring layup after layup?** This is usually more of a rhetorical question. Coaches typically have a pretty good idea why the other team is having success scoring, but their teams may not. That's sometimes the price of learning man-to-man D in a game.

It's important to keep the corrections concise, simple, and easy to understand. Start by asking the first four questions in this series. They're designed to prompt the players to start thinking about their actions on the court. Encourage the players to search their innocent souls for the answer. Sooner or later, the answers will start to sink in, and you'll be playing tough man-to-man D.

The Coach's Clipboard

✔ Defenders need to work together to prevent scores.

✔ Use zone defense as a stepping stone to teach man-to-man.

✔ Zone defenders must stay active; with each pass, all five defenders must adjust their floor position.

✔ Defenders should move to the ball while the pass is in the air.

✔ Man-to-man defenders need to see the ball and see their man at all times.

✔ Man-to-man defenders must help their teammates by staying open to the ball.

✔ Good defensive communication starts with answering the question, *Who do you have?*

✔ Man-to-man defenders must learn not to chase the ball.

✔ Instead they need to stay ahead of the ball and cut off the offensive player's path to the basket.

✔ Avoid the Red Sea effect and always have at least one or two defenders at the help line.

Special Plays and Situations

Here's the situation: A jump ball at midcourt, and your center lines up with a huge height disadvantage against the opposing center. It looks like the other team will win the tip, but does your team know how to line up to prevent a quick basket?

Five seconds left, down by a point, and you need to score off an inbounds play. But does your team even know what an inbounds play is?

One minute left, up by five, and you need to play keepaway with the ball from the other team. But does your team have an offense that can eat up some clock?

These kinds of potentially high-stress situations can wear away at a team's confidence and a coach's composure. But these and other special game situations can be handled with a minimum of stress by preparing for them in advance. Young players can't be expected to execute something in a game they have never done in practice. The main idea behind preparing for special plays is to keep things manageable. The players—and the coach—will already be stressed enough trying to run an offense and maintain a defense. So these special plays need to be simple. But they will be effective if executed properly and practiced frequently.

When in doubt, introduce the concept in practice rather than skipping it. The earlier the players are exposed to some of these ideas, the more readily they will be able to recognize them as they come up in games. You'll have more than a few of those, *Oh, now I get it!* moments from your team during the season, and this is the *Oh, now I get it!* chapter. All of the situations described here will arise in just about every game. The team might not grasp their importance right away in practice, but as they see how these situations arise in games and can affect the outcome, they'll be eager to learn as much as they can.

Jump Ball

Basketball games start with a jump ball, and that may be the only time in the game it is used. (Any overtime periods begin with a jump ball.) But it can set a tone. No team wants to give up a quick basket off the opening tip and fall instantly behind. So it's important for each team to have a jump-ball setup and a plan for what to do depending on who wins the tip.

There are two basic ways to set up for a jump ball: an offensive alignment (figure 7.1a) or a defensive alignment (figure 7.1b). If your team has a size advantage at the center position and it's highly likely you'll win the tip, use the offensive alignment. Position two players on the offensive side (near the basket you're scoring in) of the jump-ball circle, ready to receive the ball from your center. They should be on opposite sides of the imaginary help line that splits the court from basket to basket. Your two other players should line up on the defensive side. One lines up on the circle, and the other is the safety—a player positioned a few feet behind the jump-ball circle to defend your basket and prevent an easy layup off the tip.

If it's uncertain or unlikely you'll win the tip, use the defensive alignment. In addition to the center, position two players on the defensive side of the circle (on opposite sides of the help line), as well as the safety, and put only one player on the offensive side of the circle.

The priority of each player on the jump-ball circle is to secure the ball off the tip. The center cannot catch his own tip, so it's up to the other four players to battle for the ball. Running a quick scoring play off the tip is rare and should be contemplated only if the jumper has a big height advantage over the opponent. In this case, the center tips the ball toward the offensive basket in the direction of a teammate on the offensive side of the circle. If there are two players on the offensive side, the one who didn't receive the tip should break for the basket and look for a quick pass. If the team is set up defensively and unexpectedly wins the tip, look for a quick score if the other team over commits to offense and is momentarily outnumbered on defense (2 on 1 or 3 on 2). Otherwise, set up the half-court offense.

Players on the defensive side of the circle should always line up with their outside shoulders (away from the basket) against the inside shoulders (closest to the basket) of their opponents and should be ready to drop back as quickly as possibly to defend the basket. They want to avoid getting beat for a quick layup off the tip. The safety should allow

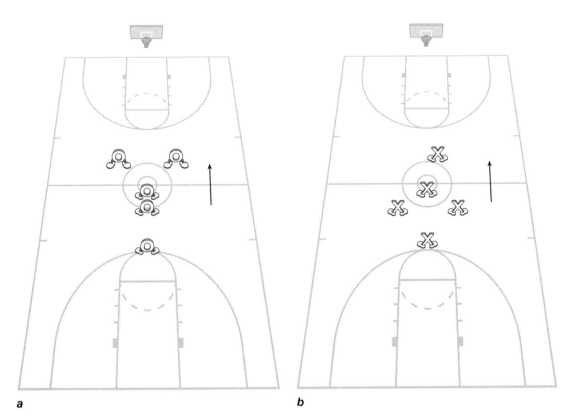

Figure 7.1   *(a)* Offensive and *(b)* defensive alignments for a jump ball.

plenty of cushion, playing at least 5 feet closer to the basket than the nearest opponent.

Out-of-Bounds Plays

The ball flies, bounces, skips, and ricochets out of bounds dozens of times during a game. Bringing the ball inbounds at the other team's end of the court actually can be pretty difficult against a tenacious defense, so it's important to have at least a couple of inbounds plays ready that can accomplish two goals: ensure that the ball is securely inbounded and provide an opportunity to score.

Before passing the ball, the inbounder needs to yell out the play. The play should not start until the inbounder slaps the ball with her palm or yells, "Break!" Otherwise, the players on the floor will make their cuts at different times and destroy the rhythm of the play. When inbounding the ball after the opponent has made a basket, it's permissible for inbounders to move around behind the baseline. But on all other inbounds plays, the passer must establish a pivot foot and avoid shuffling his feet. Under no circumstances may the inbounder cross the baseline or sideline before passing the ball.

Stack

The stack alignment is for inbounding under the offensive basket and gives the inbounder four passing options to four points on the floor. At least three of these options are designed to set up a shot relatively close to the basket. The fourth option is a safety pass to a guard near the top of the key. Players line up in a stack formation on the same side as the basketball (see figure 7.2). Four players should line up behind each other along the free-throw lane line above the low block. Players should stand an arm's length apart from each other. The position for lining up in the stack (1 is the closest to the inbounder and 2 is farthest from the ball) and each player's movements follow:

Player 3 inbounds the ball.

Player 1 breaks about 8 to 10 feet to the outside corner of the floor on the same side and looks to receive an inbounds pass for a quick outside shot.

Player 4 breaks to the opposite low block and looks for a quick pass for a layup or rebound and a second-shot opportunity.

Player 5 steps toward the inbounder and looks for a pass and a layup opportunity.

Player 2 cuts to the opening up high in the key area.

The inbounder should try to get the ball to 1, 4, or 5 for a shot. Whichever player gets open closest to the basket should get the ball. Use 2 as a safety option in case the first three options are covered. This can be confusing at first for the inbounder, but with practice, the passer will learn to see all the players as they make their breaks. It's important for the inbounder not to focus on one target, but to use peripheral vision to see all the cutters. Over time, the inbounder can learn how to decoy the defense by pretending to focus on one cutter and passing to another.

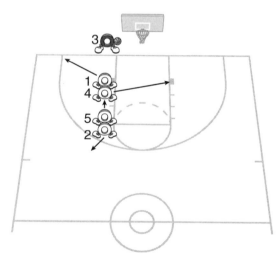

Figure 7.2 Player positions for the stack inbounds play.

Hawk

The hawk play is designed to set up a quick shot for the inbounder after the inbounds pass is made. Ideally, the inbounder for this play should be the best outside shooter on the floor. Players set up in a box on the opposite low blocks and the elbows (see figure 7.3a). Use the following player assignments and positioning:

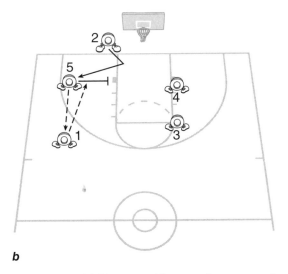

Player 2 inbounds the ball.

Player 5 sets up on the strong-side block (in front of inbounder).

Player 1 sets up on the strong-side elbow.

Player 3 sets up on the weak-side elbow.

Player 4 sets up on weak-side low block.

Player 5 cuts in toward the basket and back out to the corner to receive the inbounds pass from 2. Player 1 cuts toward the basket and out toward the wing, and 5 passes to 1. After 5 releases the pass to 1, 2 cuts toward the basket, then breaks toward the outside corner on the same side of the floor about 12 to 15 feet from the basket. After throwing the pass to 1, 5 should turn and set a screen for 2 (figure 7.3b). Player 1 passes the ball to 2, and 2 takes a shot. Player 3 floats to the opening in the key area in case 2 cannot enter the ball to 5. Player 4 breaks in under the basket for a rebound.

Figure 7.3 (a) Player positions, early movement, and (b) final movement for the hawk inbounds play.

Sideline Stack

Inbounding the ball from the sideline can be a challenge, especially if the defense is in full deny mode and itching for a steal. So it's important for the team to have a play in place to get the ball safely inbounds and set up its offense or score quickly against an overaggressive defense. This calls for an alignment similar to the stack play.

Three players line up about 8 to 10 feet from the sideline, directly across from the inbounder and about 4 to 5 feet from one another, as shown in figure 7.4. Player 4 aligns directly across from the inbounder near the opposite sideline. The play is designed to allow player 2 to score a quick basket on a pass from 5.

Figure 7.4 Setup and initial action for sideline stack.

- **Player 5** inbounds the ball.
- **Player 2** sets a screen for 1, then cuts toward the basket (after 3 sets a screen for 2; figure 7.5) looking for a pass from 5.
- **Player 1** comes off the screen and looks for a pass from 5.
- **Player 3** sets a screen for 2.
- **Player 4** runs down the floor toward the basket and looks for a pass from 2.

The success of this play depends on the players having the patience to set the screens in the proper sequence. Player 2 must screen for 1 before 3 screens for 2. Remember that the inbounder has five seconds to make the pass before a violation is called and the ball is turned over to the opponent. If the players rush through the play, they'll end up colliding and nullifying the effect of the screens.

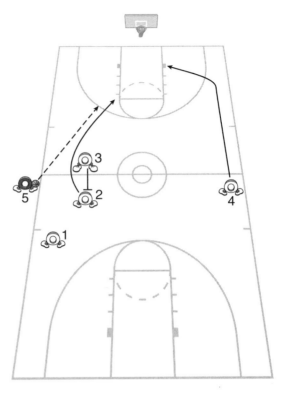

Figure 7.5 Triple-screen sidelines stack play.

Team and Individual Fouls

Fouling the opponent is usually something to be discouraged, but sometimes it is a sound strategy for a team trying to overcome a lead as time is running down. In many youth leagues, when a team has reached a certain number of team fouls in a half (usually seven), the opposing team is awarded a one-and-one free-throw shot opportunity on all nonshooting fouls. Before that number is reached, a nonshooting foul results in the ball being awarded out of bounds to your opponent, and there is no change of possession. One-and-one means that the shooting team must make the first free throw before being awarded a second attempt. If the first free throw is missed, the ball is live. (Note that in some leagues and tournaments, 10 team fouls will result in two free throws, even on nonshooting violations, with the ball becoming live after the second attempt.)

The number of team fouls can be an important factor near the end of a close game. The team that is losing will want to foul to stop the clock and get to the maximum number of team fouls so that the winning team will have to shoot free throws. This puts the pressure on the team in the lead to make the first free throw. The losing team will get more opportunities to get a rebound and try to go back down the floor and score to cut the lead. Of course, this strategy doesn't work if the team in the lead is making its free throws, but it's worth a try to regain possession of the ball.

So, when to foul? If a team is losing and the game is out of reach, it's pointless to foul. But if the margin is less than 10 points with about three minutes left, defenders on the trailing team should go for steals and foul if they fail to get the ball. Keep in mind that usually defenders who don't go for the ball while fouling will be called for an intentional foul, and the other team will be awarded free throws and possession of the ball. So, make sure your players know the proper way to foul in this situation. Believe it or not, it's difficult for many players to grasp the concept of fouling as a strategy. So it's something that should be discussed and worked on in practice. When a coach yells *Take one!* in a game, the defensive team should be able to commit a quick foul to stop the clock.

A coach also needs to manage individual fouls to keep players from fouling out. Each game usually will have a scorekeeper who keeps track of the score and the individual fouls. In most games, players are allotted four fouls each. On the fifth foul, the player is out of the game. So if a player picks up two fouls in the first half, the coach will want to get that player out of the game to avoid picking up a third foul before halftime. Similarly, if a player picks up a quick third foul at the outset of the second half, the coach may want to get the player out of the game to avoid a fourth foul with nearly half the game left. Before the game, the coach should ask the scorekeeper to speak up whenever a player draws a second, third, or fourth foul. If a coach is fortunate enough to have an assistant, one of the assistant's main jobs should be to stay on top of the foul situation.

Free Throws

Fouls go hand-in-hand with free throws. There usually are plenty of both in youth-league games, so it's important to prepare your players for what will happen once the referee's whistle blows, a foul is called, and a player goes to the foul line to shoot. Rebounders line up along the free-throw lane lines and must be aware of how many free throws have been awarded to the shooter and be ready to rebound any missed shots once the ball is in play. The rebounders must be aware of the rules on where they can stand (outside the free-throw lane) and when they can enter the free-throw lane (only after the ball hits the rim on the free-throw attempt).

Players are awarded two free throws on all shooting fouls. But usually starting with the seventh team foul in each half, the other team begins shooting free throws even on nonshooting fouls (usually a *one-and-one,* in which the player is entitled to a second free throw only if the first free throw is made; if the first free throw is missed, the ball is live).

The distance between the foul line and the front of the rim in most games is 13 feet. But this can be a daunting distance for younger players. In certain younger leagues, the rules may call for a shorter distance to give players a more realistic chance of making free throws. Ideally, players should be able to shoot free throws from a distance that does not require them to drastically alter their shot just to reach the rim. In certain instances, the opposing coaches and referees may agree before the game to shorten the distance for free throws. In any case, it's important for the coach to know what the league rules allow and then to have the players shoot free throws from game distance during practice.

Shooting Free Throws

Free-throw shooting can be intimidating for basketball novices, so start with the basics. Explain to your players that no matter how far away the free-throw line is, the shooter cannot cross the line until the ball has touched the rim. This can be an issue in younger leagues if the kids don't have the strength to get the basketball to the goal. Younger players may need to jump to get the ball anywhere close to the rim. In this case, caution them to adjust their position on the line accordingly so they don't finish their jump across the line. If the ball misses the rim completely on the second free throw of a shooting foul or on either attempt of a one-and-one, the ball is dead and the other team is awarded the ball out of bounds. As the players mature and get stronger, they are usually able to shoot free throws from a stationary position with both feet on the floor.

Whether players shoot from a jump or a stationary position, proper shooting technique should be encouraged. This is the one shot during the game that the players can completely control, and the shooter should learn to take his time and follow the same routine every time: focus on the target (just above the rim), steady the feet (about shoulder-width apart), relax the shoulders with a deep breath, adjust the hands so they are gripping the ball properly along the seams, and then coil and finish with a smooth, high follow-through.

Rebounding Missed Free Throws on Offense

Teams line up for the rebound along both free-throw lane lines. The shooting team is allowed to have one player on each side of the lane to contest the rebound. These players should usually be the tallest players (4 and 5). The offensive players line up next to the opponent's rebounder in the low block on each side of the lane. None of the rebounders can cross the line into the lane to grab a rebound until the free throw has touched the rim. If the free throw is good but the offensive team jumps into the lane too early, the referee will take away the point and award the ball out of bounds to the other team.

The other two offensive players must stand behind the three-point line while the free throw is being shot and be ready to drop back quickly on defense. Their main job is to prevent a fast break and a quick layup after a missed free throw. Once the free-throw shooter takes her shot and the ball hits the rim, she should step into the lane and try to get a rebound. Sometimes the ball takes a long bounce back to the shooter and presents an opportunity for a quick score.

Rebounding Missed Free Throws on Defense

A team that commits a foul that results in a free throw now has one major goal: Get the ball back. The worst thing that can happen is for the free-throw shooting team to rebound their own miss and get a quick basket or start running their offense again. So it's imperative that the defense work on rebounding missed free throws in practice.

The order of defensive players along each lane line is as follows (see figure 7.6): The tallest players from the defensive team should occupy the low-block positions (4 and 5). Of course, next in line on each side is a player from the shooter's team. Third in line are two more defensive players (2 and 3). The last member of the defense, usually a guard (1), must be positioned outside the three-point arc. Except for the players aligned along the line and the shooter, no player from either team can be inside the arc while a free throw is being shot. All the players on the floor must hold their positions until the ball hits the rim. If the defensive team crosses the lane lines early, the shooter will be awarded another free throw.

The defense's main objective is to secure the rebound. Instead of jumping at the ball, 4 and 5 must first step in front of the opposing player next to them and box out. They should step into the lane toward the free-throw shooter with their outside leg and seal off the opposing rebounder with their body. Then they need to jump

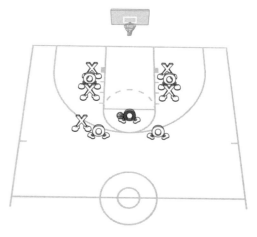

Figure 7.6 Correct lineup of players for a free throw.

and meet the ball as high as possible with outstretched hands after it bounces off the rim.

Either 2 or 3 must box out the shooter to prevent a long offensive rebound off a miss. The two players must communicate and one of them must call "shooter" before the free throw is attempted to indicate which one will step into the lane and box out the shooter after the shot hits the rim.

Once the rebound is secured, the team needs to switch into offensive mode and should try to get the ball down the floor as quickly as possible for a score. This is called a *fast break*.

Fast Break

Before running the fast break, players need to learn how to run a half-court offense, and this requires control. At first, dribbling and passing will take a lot of concentration from the kids. In these early days, the toughest job for a coach is to get the players to slow down and focus on offense. Kids have energy to burn, and they'll want to fly around the court like wayward pinballs. The kids need to learn when it's time to slow down and when it's time to run. As players develop their ballhandling and passing skills, they will be able to play the game under control (relatively speaking) at a faster pace. At that point, they are ready to run a fast break.

The fast break is a fun way to play offense: It puts immense pressure on the defense to get back, it can create mismatches with two offensive players against one defender (or 3 on 2, 4 on 3, or 5 on 4), and it can lead to easy scores off layups. The team that knows how to run and score off the fast break has a tremendous advantage over a team that walks the ball down the floor every time.

While the fast break definitely speeds the game up, it still requires control. It usually is best run after a missed shot by the opposing team. Once the rebound is secured in or around the lane, the rebounder (5) should pivot out on his outside foot at about a 45-degree angle to the nearest sideline.

A ballhandler (1) should quickly pop out to an outlet area on the side of the floor nearest the rebounder. This area is about 15 feet up the floor, 10 feet or so from the elbow (*free-throw line extended* in basketball parlance). Player 1 needs to get to this area to open up a clear lane for the outlet pass (figure 7.7) from the rebounder because the defense is usually clustered near the lane. The player who rebounds the missed shot should pivot away from the middle of the court and look outside for the outlet pass. After securing the pass, player 1 should dribble the ball as quickly as possible toward the middle of the floor. Two offensive players

(2 and 4) should sprint up the floor as close as possible to opposite sidelines, filling lanes on either side of 1.

Player 1 should push the ball up the floor as far as possible and may even be able to go the distance for a layup if no one gets back in time on defense. If 1 encounters a defender, 1 can take a short outside shot if the defender plays back or pass to 2 or 4 if the defender commits to stopping 1. As they sprint down the floor, 2 and 4 should stay as wide as possible, at least 10 to 15 feet apart from 1, to spread out the defense and create a good passing angle. One of the biggest mistakes young fast-breakers make is run-

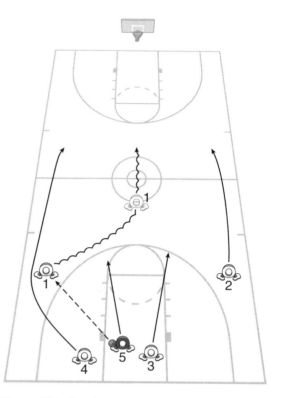

Figure 7.7   Fast-break movement.

ning straight down the middle of the floor, which makes the defense's job a lot easier (one defender can guard two offensive players) and makes the angles for the passer a lot tighter and tougher. Once 2 and 4 reach the opposing free-throw line area, they should cut toward the gates (above the low block in the free-throw lane) and look for a pass and a layup opportunity.

Players 3 and 5 should trail the play but sprint up the floor and look for rebound opportunities. If the defense gets back quickly and stops the fast break, the offense should not force the pass or shot, but try to set up the normal half-court offense.

Last-Second Shot

If it's the end of the game and you need to score to tie or go ahead, it's important to know how much time is left to play and run a play accordingly. Most young players won't be strong enough to launch, much less make, a long shot. Many won't even be aware of how much time is left in the game unless the coach reminds them.

Off an inbounds play that requires you to go the length of the court, your best bet for a quick shot is to run a variation of the give-and-go (chapter 3, page 70) off the inbounds pass. The player (2) who receives the inbounds pass should make a quick return pass to the inbounder (1), who then drives the length of the floor toward the basket. The player may be able to drive for a layup or shot in the lane, but if not, the player should try to dribble the ball to the middle of the floor. Two teammates (3 and 4) should run ahead of 1 on opposite sides of the court, each about 15 feet apart from 1, to spread the defense and look for a pass. The two remaining players (2 and 5) should trail the play and look to get open for an outside shot if the first wave is stopped by the defense or to grab a rebound and quickly score if 1, 3, or 4 are able to take a shot.

If you are underneath the opponent's basket on the inbounds play, run the stack or hawk plays. Both are designed to produce quick-hitting scores.

Stalling

The games in which your team is blowing out the opponent are the easy ones to finish. The white-knucklers are the games that are close and you are several precious minutes from the end. The losing team is doing everything it can to get the ball back. Your team's job is to play keepaway: stalling.

It's difficult for a coach—let alone a young, inexperienced team—to stay cool in such circumstances. At times like this, it helps for the coach to look confident and talk in measured tones. Verbal and physical cues from the person in charge can affect the entire team's mood and performance. It's probably not a good idea to sit with your head in your hands while muttering Marlon Brando-isms from *Apocalypse Now*: "The horror, the horror." So keep calm, Coach.

Make sure the best ballhandlers and free-throw shooters are in the game. The team that is losing will start fouling and try to force a turnover with ball pressure. Now is the time for your team to run its stall offense (see four out, one in on pages 116-117). Keep moving the ball. Make the defense work. Maintain poise. And watch those minutes crawl by.

In the four-out, one-in offense, the weak-side wing needs to move toward the screen being set at the foul line to shake off the defender, and then out to the opposite wing to receive a pass from the strong-side corner. The defense must come out from underneath the basket to retrieve the ball, and this creates more space for passing and cutting. The offense should keep the ball moving from side to side of the court with quick, short passes and dribble the ball only if absolutely necessary. Four out, one in is most effective if the players maintain proper spacing. If each player is at least 12 to 15 feet away from the nearest teammate, the defense will have to do a lot of chasing after the ball, particularly if the offense does a good job of keeping the ball moving with quick passes.

The coach should instruct the team, *No shots unless you have a wide-open layup.* Other key words include *patience* and *slow down.* Even then, some of your players will forget what they're supposed to be doing the second the game resumes and launch a 20-footer, even though your team doesn't need to score. Again, consider it a teaching opportunity. Young players usually think of only two things while in the game: *When do I get a chance to score?* and, *What's the postgame snack?* Stalling and clock awareness are disciplines that can be simulated in practice, but can be truly learned only by actually playing lots of close games.

One way to cut down on the pressure in the final minutes and keep the players focused on the task at hand is to get them to think of stalling as a game of five-person keepaway. Suddenly, the prospect of sitting on the ball turns into something fun. Imagine seeing five kids with big smiles on their faces as they toss the ball around at the end of a tight, high-pressure contest.

Full-Court Press

The full-court press usually isn't allowed in younger leagues, but it will become an issue as players get a little older. Most youth leagues don't allow defenders to press until players are about 12 years old. Others begin pressing with players as young as 9 to 10 years of age at certain times of the game only. But young players can't start learning soon enough how to dribble and pass the ball under pressure. And there is no more pressure-filled situation than when the entire court is jammed with defenders intent on creating a steal or preventing the offense from crossing half-court in 10 seconds (which results in a change of possession). Players trying to handle the ball under such circumstances invariably panic at first. But focus them on a few key fundamentals, and they can break a press:

- **Pass the ball.** After catching the ball, the offensive players must turn and face the defense and see the entire floor. As the defense approaches, the ballhandler needs to get rid of the ball with a quick pass to an open teammate.

- **Keep the ball away from the sidelines.** Players should not dribble toward the sidelines, where the out-of-bounds line can function as an extra defender. The offense should strive to keep the ball in the middle of the floor as much as possible.

- **Maintain good court spacing.** If the offense clusters, the defense can easily swarm to the ball. If the offensive players maintain 12 to 15 feet between each other, the defense will have to spread out and the driving lanes in the floor will open up. If the defense tries to double-team the ball, proper spacing should make it easy for a teammate to get open.

The defense needs time to set up a press, usually after a dead ball or a basket. So the more quickly the offensive team retrieves the basketball and gets it in play, the less time the defense has to set up their press. But if the opponent's press is set up, your team must recognize what type of press they are facing and react accordingly. The offense must be prepared to break two kinds of presses: a zone press and a man-to-man press.

Defeating a Zone Press

The zone press comes in different sizes. Box and one (2-2-1) and diamond and one (1-2-1-1) are among the most common. The offense uses a similar approach to break both: Two guards (1 and 2) line up at the free-throw line. Two forwards (3 and 4) position themselves on opposite sides of the half-court line. A forward/center (5) inbounds the ball (figure 7.8).

1 and 2 split and move into open areas. The ball is entered to 1, and the weak-side forward (3) moves to an open spot in the middle of the floor. Player 2 floats out and up the weak side of the floor. Player 5 steps inbounds immediately and positions himself in the middle of the floor about 10 to 15 feet away and slightly behind 1 for a possible return pass. Player 4 moves down the floor looking for a pass and a layup. The basketball can now be passed from the strong side of the floor to the middle, and then to the weak side.

Figure 7.8   A strategy for breaking two common types of the zone press.

Coaching Points

The guard who receives the inbounds pass should turn and face the floor rather than dribbling the ball; a zone defense is designed to trap dribblers. Each offensive player who handles the ball against a zone press should strive to move the ball with quick passes. They should look to the middle or weak side and keep moving the ball up the floor.

Defeating a Man-to-Man Press

The strategy for breaking the man-to-man is slightly different. Whereas beating a zone requires patience and passing, beating a man-to-man is more about screening and getting the ball in the hands of the team's most reliable ballhandlers.

Players 2 and 3 line up at the weak-side elbow on the opposite side of the lane from the inbound passer (5). Players 2 and 3 set up a *double-stack screen*, with 2 closest to the inbounder. In a double-stack screen, the screeners line up one behind each other and face the point guard (1). Player 1 lines up on the weak side about 10 to 12 feet from the screeners. Player 4 lines up at midcourt on the strong side (figure 7.9).

Player 1 curls around the double-stack screen toward the ball side and looks for the inbounds pass. Player 1 then dribbles up the floor; the main objective is to get the ball past half court to avoid a 10-second violation. After setting a screen, 2 peels off opposite 1 and presents a second option for 5 to inbound the ball if 1 is covered. After setting a screen, 3 runs up the floor looking for a pass from 1. Player 4 runs up the floor on the sideline opposite 3. Player 1 works the ball to the middle of the floor and looks for a fast-break opportunity.

Another option, known as a *fly pattern*, for beating the man-to-man press is to create a quick scoring opportunity with a long pass. This will apply only to teams with a player who can throw the ball to at least half-court on the fly. This can quickly be determined in practice. In this play, 2 lines up behind 1 at about the free-throw line. As

Figure 7.9   The double-stack screen.

Coaching Points

The point guard must run the defender into the double-stack screen and curl off the shoulders of the screeners to shake off defenders and receive the inbounds pass. If the guard leaves too much space between himself and the screeners, defenders can easily slip through the gap and prevent the guard from getting the pass. The point guard turns upcourt immediately after receiving the inbounds pass and keeps her head up, looking to the weak side first for a scoring opportunity.

shown in figure 7.10, players 3 and 4 line up near the sidelines at opposite ends of the midcourt line. On the signal of the inbounder (5), 3 and 4 break toward their respective corners nearest the inbounder to draw the defenders away from half-court. 2 cuts toward 5 to draw the defender forward, then curls around 1 and runs upcourt while looking over the shoulder for a pass. Player 5 throws a football-style pass to 2, who then dribbles in for a layup.

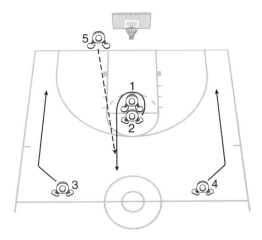

Figure 7.10   The fly pattern.

Time-Outs

Time-outs are the most important tool a coach has during the game. They can be used to change the momentum, set up offensive plays, switch defenses, create last-second scoring opportunities, or give the team a breather. Time-outs are precious and they must be managed. Check with the league or tournament rules so you know how many time-outs each team is allotted.

Usually, only a minute or two is allotted per time-out, so a coach needs to be organized before calling the time-out. Your dry-erase board will come in handy. Players just love visuals, especially when they're having trouble remembering plays. A quick drawing can rest your worn-out voice and help the team quickly visualize where each player needs to position herself on the floor. By the way, drawing up Xs and Os on the board doesn't require any artistic technique, but it might be helpful to practice at home ahead of time. Draw up all the plays the team has learned at home a few times so that it's second nature during the game.

In the few seconds you have for the time-out, have something specific to tell the team, get to the point, and keep it simple. Make the team aware of one or two main points that you want them to take to the floor. If you try to cram too much information into such a tight space, the players will end up forgetting most of it. You want them to leave the huddle with purpose and inspiration, not confusion and *What did he just say?* looks in their eyes. Players will often be too shy to admit they're confused, so it can be helpful to ask the team to repeat the main points before they go out on the floor: *Run the stack out-of-bounds play. On defense, we need to move our feet more and stop reaching with our hands for steals.*

Make sure the team hustles in from the floor, because you don't have much time, and that players grab their water bottles before joining the huddle. The entire team—not just the players on the floor—should cluster around the coach. Everyone should hear what the coach has to say, and everyone should feel part of the team. Make it clear that time-outs are a time for the coach, and only the coach, to speak. Everyone else needs to listen.

Never single out a player for criticism. This is not the time for that. Stay positive. The players are looking for direction about what they need to do next, not a summary of what they've done wrong. As stressful as the game may be, the coach should try to keep the tone calm and reassuring. Most of the time, the players will already be excited enough without the coach adding to the hysteria. Speak authoritatively and clearly, but don't yell. Motivate, don't deflate.

Don't burn your allotment of time-outs early in the game. For example, don't waste a time-out by calling one only a few seconds before the end of the first half. But if your team comes out flat and is falling behind quickly early in the game, you may need to call a time-out to get the team back on track. Always be sure to save a few time-outs for the end of a game; in a close game, time-outs can make a critical difference in organizing the team and setting up plays.

The Coach's Clipboard

✔ Prepare for high-stress special game situations in practice.

✔ On the jump ball, make securing the ball and preventing the quick basket your top priorities.

✔ Timing is everything on out-of-bounds plays, so no one should move until the inbounder says, "Break!"

✔ Pay attention to individual and team fouls; they can be a big factor in the outcome.

✔ Free-throw shooters should have a routine they follow every time.

✔ Rebounding the free throw requires a coordinated effort, with players stepping into the lane to box out the low posts and the shooter.

✔ For a successful fast break, offensive players need to spread out and fill lanes rather than run in a cluster down the middle of the court.

✔ Stalling requires patience and spreading the floor.

✔ Quick passes, spacing the floor, and staying away from the sidelines are keys to breaking the press.

✔ Time-outs need to be managed, just like players.

Game Time! What's My Role Again?

Coaches like to think they have a certain amount of control over what happens on the basketball floor—and to an extent, they do. A coach can script a practice so that she has a pretty good idea of what's going to happen when she walks in the gym: Some kids will fidget; others will pay attention. Some will execute the drills well; others will fumble around. But in general, everyone will be on the same page, following the coach's direction down to the minute. The more organized the coach is, the more in control she'll be, and practice will run smoothly, despite a few unexpected slip-ups here and there.

Games are a different story. It's not quite chaos, but it can come uncomfortably close at times, especially with a fledgling team getting its first taste of competition, complete with uniforms, a scoreboard, referees, and Mom and Dad cheering in the stands. The toughest thing for a new coach to realize is that once the game starts, his role actually diminishes. It's up to the kids now.

We've seen this happen a few million times: The coach will call a time-out, pull out the handy dry-erase board, draw up a beautifully designed yet simple play that the team has been practicing for weeks, and send the team out to run it. Then the team promptly runs a completely different play, or two players run the play the coach designed while three other players stand dumbfounded, or the group doesn't run much of anything at all.

At moments like this, you'll be tempted to close your eyes and start muttering to yourself. Do not be discouraged. Do not curse the day you took this sometimes thankless job. Instead, try to remember what it felt like to be eight years old, without a care in the world. Then, during the next break in the action, draw up the same play and urge your eager minions to try, try again.

Early in the season, you'll be tempted to try to correct everything at once, because everything will seem wrong. But it's best to work on one thing at a time. You will find yourself repeating the same points many times. You will find yourself straining your creativity as you try to find new and exciting ways to say the same thing. But rest assured that after about 21 repetitions, some of what you say will sink in.

Even if it doesn't, resist the temptation to act out. Although it's tempting, coaches can't throw on a uniform and play the game for their team. Those uniforms wouldn't fit anyway. So coaches are left to pace the sideline, where they sometimes resort to fretting, screaming, and pulling out what's left of their hair. That sort of dramatic display might work for the TV cameras at an NBA game, but hissy fits just won't cut it in a youth basketball game.

If you must suffer, Coach, suffer in silence. Your players will actually play better if you keep your comments to a minimum. If you do feel the need to comment, keep it positive. Your job is to be their guide, not their micromanager. Embrace that attitude, and you immediately cut your acid indigestion by 50 percent. Your players, and your stomach, will thank you.

At times, you might need to have a conversation with a player who is showing a little negative attitude, but it's important that the conversation be kept constructive, positive, and private. Some young players will test a new authority figure in their lives to see how far they can push things, but when they're gently but firmly shown the boundaries, they usually back off and get with the team's program.

Even as the season progresses, recognize that kids will continue to be kids, and they will occasionally revert to running around like the proverbial beheaded chickens. At such moments, have a laugh, shake your head in appreciation of the follies of youth, and call a time-out to gather all your Chicken Littles for a brief refresher course in the game of basketball.

Defining Your Role

In many ways the game is the most anxious time of all for a new coach. It's the moment when you feel that you are on public display, when your hard work in practice will be ruthlessly judged by the parents, the opposing coaches and players, the referees, and even your own team. You're nervous about being exposed as a fraud or embarrassed by the opposition. It's normal to feel that way, but it's an insecurity you can overcome. How? By defining your role ahead of time.

Every coach must be able to answer one question before stepping on the court: What is the ultimate goal? Your role goes far beyond the basketball court. The way you speak to and interact with the players can make a huge difference in how they play. A positive experience is what everyone wants, but sometimes the desire to win overtakes the more noble approach. No doubt, we all want to win. But how to define winning? Is it by the numbers on the scoreboard? If the team wins a game, but five players are crying at the end because they never played, no coach should be celebrating.

The main urge a coach needs to control at game time is the desire to micromanage every little movement on the court. The players are so busy focusing on the task at hand—whether it's dribbling the ball or defending an opponent—that additional words from the sideline, even by a respected authority figure, can be more of a hindrance than a help in the heat of a game. Save the verbal feedback for the players when they are on the bench and can focus on what you're saying. Even then, keep your words short and to the point. Save the speeches for your lavish Coach of the Year award banquet.

Brief instructions that require specific actions—*More passing, less dribbling, Get to the help line more quickly, Drive to the basket,* etc.—will help your team most. And not all at once. One or two specific instructions at a time is about all the advice new players will be able to understand and execute in the hurly-burly of a game.

That's not to say a coach should sit passively through a game and merely observe. How you act in a tight, hard-fought game can have a profound effect on the players' performance, not only in the moment but in future games. The key isn't just what the coaches say, but how and when they say it. Shouting *Come on!* or *What was that?* won't help. Those kinds of exasperated critiques will only further confuse the players and put them on edge: *A grown-up is yelling at me, but I don't know why.*

Keep the commands brief, simple and specific: *Help line! Slow it down! Sprint! No fouls! Drive!* And try to keep those thoughts of *Why did I take this job?* to yourself if at all possible. They will creep into your head, and they need to be killed on contact. Don't worry. Your team will make a good play eventually, and suddenly your entire being will be filled with happiness: *I love this game!*

Managing Pregame Details

Before you talk to your team about the specifics of playing the game, take care of a few essential tasks. These may seem mundane, even distracting, but they're critical for ensuring that the game is played in an orderly and, above all, safe manner.

- Add your player roster and player numbers to the scorebook. Keep a copy of the roster with you so you can quickly copy it for all games.

- Check that all players are wearing kneepads and that their jerseys are tucked in. Players who forget their kneepads should not play without knee protection. As a last resort, have them borrow pads from a player on the bench and return them when they come out of the game.

- Look to see that no one is wearing jewelry, bracelets, or metal hair clips. Use tape to cover up pierced-ear studs if they can't be removed easily.

- Ensure that every child has brought water for the game. Always have a few extra dollars in your wallet to buy a drink from a beverage machine or concession stand for a player who has forgotten to bring water. Locate any nearby drinking fountains that the players can use.

- Remind all players to take a bathroom break in plenty of time before the opening tip-off.

- Greet the opposing coach and referees. Identify yourself and wish everyone a good game. A brief, friendly icebreaker conversation with the adults supervising the game will help create an atmosphere of cooperation. Yes, you're there to compete, but not at the expense of sportsmanship and safety. If a dispute arises in the game, you'll all be better equipped to deal with it in a civil manner.

- Ensure the scorer's table is staffed. The referees may ask you to enlist a parent to run the scoreboard or keep the scorebook (keeping track of the individual scoring and team fouls). These are relatively simple tasks, but they may require a minute or two of training. The referees usually handle these little primers before the game with the volunteer scorekeepers, but coaches should familiarize themselves with these tasks as well.

- Ask the scorekeeper to inform you about individual and team fouls so that you can better manage your substitutions.

Managing the Game Positively

Coaches arrive at the gym on game day full of anticipation and anxiety. What are you going to say to your team? How are you going to keep them focused once the game gets rolling and the nerves kick in? It's best to think before you get to the gym about what you want to tell your team. Plot out the things you want to convey and how, so that you can keep things simple and to the point. Weed out everything that isn't absolutely necessary to convey.

The following list provides the essentials of what you'll need to communicate to the team before the game:

- **The starting lineup.** You'll want to prepare the lineup ahead of time so you aren't fumbling for names seconds before tip-off. Coaches will be tempted to start their best players and sub in the weaker players all the time. But in youth basketball, it's much more important to give every player a chance to experience being a starter, so rotate the lineup every game.

- **Defensive set and court direction.** If you're playing man-to-man, make sure each player knows which opponent he's going to cover. If you're playing zone, make sure players know the zone set and what area they are to cover. Remember to use your dry-erase board. In addition, be sure your players know which way they are going on offense and which basket they will be defending. It's not as easy as it looks.

- **Out-of-bounds plays.** Review the out-of-bounds plays with the team on your board. Remind them that the player inbounding the basketball is responsible for calling the play, but that you will help them out during the game with timely reminders

- **Pep talk.** It's always a good idea to remind the players what's coming up. It's a game. The object is to have fun. There's no reason to be nervous or scared. But there is one requirement: Play hard. Mistakes will be made, but every player, no matter what her ability, needs to play with energy and passion. That means hustling back on defense, diving on the floor for loose balls (while wearing kneepads, of course), scrapping for rebounds, and loudly encouraging teammates.

- **Question-and-answer time.** Give the players a chance to ask questions. Inevitably, one of the kids will ask, *What's the postgame snack?* Reveal this top-secret information if you feel it will give your team more incentive to play well, then encourage questions related to the actual game itself. If your players are new to the game, chances are they won't even know what to ask. All you can do at this point is to offer the most timeless advice available: *All right, then, go out there, play hard, and have fun!*

Remember, the players will also be nervous and excited, so the more you talk, the less they will actually hear. Parents know that glazed-eye look their own kids give them mid-speech. At a certain point, the little rascals just tune out. So don't expect your players to be riveted on your every profound thought, especially when they've got a game to play. In as succinct a fashion as possible, give the players the minimum information they need to do a good job. Keep it simple. Keep it brief.

During the game, the coach's primary job is to encourage and support the players. Keep smiling, and dish out compliments like Halloween candy. Enjoy the effort, even if it's misguided. Applaud the hustle, even when ineptitude breaks out like a bad rash. Don't raise your voice unless it's to be heard above the noise in the gym, and then only to say something positive. When a player comes out of the game hanging her head after a bad play, take each negative and turn it into a positive teaching opportunity: "Good try, Melissa! That was a great effort. Just be sure next time to move your feet instead of reaching for the ball, and you'll stop them every time."

Winning is always a welcome outcome, but it shouldn't override the coach's main concerns. It's easy to lose sight of what's important as the game progresses and the competitive juices start flowing. But most of your team won't lose any sleep later that night over who won or lost, and neither should you. Instead, put your energy into three must-do tasks during the game:

1. **Keep it fun.** It's not about winning at all costs. If all the kids aren't having fun, we all lose. The key to this is making sure everyone plays and everyone has an opportunity to contribute, no matter what their level of talent. You can do this by focusing on effort, hustle, and teamwork, and de-emphasizing the score. If the kids are trying hard, that's all you can ask. Even as the mistakes pile up, keep smiling and keep teaching. Don't wag a finger and scold the kids for messing up plays and concepts they've only just begun to learn. Always reward effort with applause, high fives, and pats on the back. Not only is it OK to crack a smile and even tell a joke occasionally, it is a must-do.

2. **Put players in positions to succeed.** Know your players' abilities, and coach accordingly. For example, don't put your slowest player in a game to guard the other team's best ballhandler. Don't expect a small guard to score against a much bigger defender. Don't make players throw 40-foot passes when their bodies can produce only 10-foot passes.

    Emphasize to your team that a player who gets open near the basket should get the ball. Set goals that the players can reach individually and as a team. Challenge weaker players to do something as simple as trying to drive to the basket with their off hand or moving to the help line quickly as a help-side defender. Conversely, challenge your stronger players, without naming names, to include all their teammates when they pass the ball. Reward them when they get the ball to a player near the basket for a layup, even if the layup is missed. Encourage small achievements that can be built on over a season.

3. **Make substitutions and keep track of playing time.** Coaches will be tempted to play their best players most of the time, but it's critical to get the entire bench involved. Work the substitutes in one by one so that the weaker players aren't on the floor all at once without any support from the stronger players. By playing the best players at key moments of the game (the beginning and end of each half), a team can remain competitive without leaving out its bench players. Work in substitutes during the middle section of each half, and take players out every three to five minutes. This will keep the players on the bench focused on the game, because they will know they're going to play soon.

It can be a daunting task figuring out when to substitute. Share this responsibility with an assistant if one is available. Playing time should be as equal as you can possibly make it, but it's difficult, if not impossible, to precisely monitor the minutes of 10 to 12 players. Despite a coach's best efforts, some players will still be shortchanged. If so, coaches should acknowledge the oversight to the player (and to the players' parents if they're in attendance) and try to redress the balance in subsequent games.

Good sportsmanship should prevail from the beginning of the game to the end. After the game, no matter what the outcome, line up and shake hands with the other team and coaches. Then meet with the team in private and explain what they did well and what they need to work on. Encourage them to work at home on areas of the game they may be struggling to master, such as free throws, layups, and ballhandling. Do not single out individual players, except for praise. Keep the focus on the team. Set times for the next practices and games.

Minimizing Moping and Gloating

We all want to win, but nobody wins all the time. Teaching young players how to lose with dignity and win with grace can be a tough task. Coaches have the power to show how it's done. No matter how good a coach thinks his team is, there is likely another team out there that is better. And no matter how bad a coach thinks his team is, there is probably another team out there that is worse. So, don't wring your hands over outcomes. Don't fret about the score. Don't reach for the antacid every time a bigger, faster opponent is on the schedule. Don't worry about factors that can't be controlled: the superhuman skills of the other team, the quality of the officiating, the lack of decent hot dog vendors at the gym. Focus on teaching the game, no matter how far behind or ahead you are in the game.

There is a natural tendency for coaches to stop coaching when their team is losing badly. They sit down and stop talking to their players because they feel the loss is a reflection on them, and they want to become invisible. Get over it. Even Dean Smith got his butt whipped in hundreds of basketball games, with far better talent than most youth-league coaches will ever have on their bench.

Difficult as it may be to accept, the best lessons are often learned when a team is getting pounded. A game filled with mistakes isn't cause for bleak thoughts; it's a bounty of teaching opportunities. Not to get all Pollyannaish here, but each screw-up is the basketball equivalent of an eager student raising a hand in class and firing off a wrong answer. You've got to love the effort, if not the result.

So the coach's response to the blown pass should not be: *How the heck could you do that?* Instead, try *Hey, I love the drive to the basket, but do you know why your pass was intercepted? You looked right at the person you were going to pass to and gave the defense a chance to recover and make the steal. Next time, don't hesitate, and you'll make a great play. I know you can do it.* Suddenly, a negative situation doesn't look so depressing. It becomes a jumping-off point for the next practice, where the coaching point can be re-emphasized, this time with an example from the most recent game.

Sometimes, a coach can be at a loss for words during a game that is going badly and quickly becoming worse. At halftime, it can be apparent to everyone, including the janitor waiting to mop up afterward, that the game is already over. But here's a way to salvage something out of what looks like nothing. At halftime, tell the team to start the game over, and keep a new score for the second half. Their goal should be to make the second half a better game, a game they might even win. A negative becomes a positive. Always give the team an incentive to play well, rather than dwelling on past mistakes. Reward hustle and effort. Those factors alone can bring a team back from a big deficit and instill confidence for the next game.

What if the tables are reversed, and the basketball gods have given the team an ultra-easy game to win? Say you're up by 15 points and the game is well in hand. Here are some changes you can make to keep things from getting out of hand and embarrassing the other team.

- Stop playing man-to-man and switch to a zone defense. This usually lets the other team take some outside shots.
- Skip the fast breaks to cut down on easy layups. Walk the ball up and try running a half-court offense. Tell the team to make at least five passes before attempting a shot.
- Even if your league allows it, don't use a full-court press. This will give the other team a chance to get the basketball into a half-court set and try to run their offense.

You may not win as easily by playing this way, but you'll win the respect of everyone in the gym. And maybe the good faith will be returned the next time your team is on the receiving end of a whipping. Even if it's not, continue to play with good sportsmanship in blowout victories.

Working With Referees

Despite what some fans think, basketball couldn't exist without referees. No disrespect to the coaches, but the referees often have the toughest job in the gym: They have to keep order in a house with 10 kids chasing a ball while a bunch of adults yell and cheer. All respect is due to the men and women in the striped shirts; they make the sometimes unpopular calls so the game has life.

Generally, most referees will answer civilized questions about a call they have made. Yelling usually does not endear you to the referee and can sometimes hurt the team as borderline calls start going against you. Approach referees with respect; they're adults trying to do their jobs to the best of their ability, too. In addition, as the ranking authority figure on a team, you have a responsibility to keep cool. If the coach yells and screams, the players will think it's OK for them to behave with a similar lack of decorum.

Emphasize respect. The players should never question a referee's decision. They must learn to play through adversity, including so-called "bad" calls. Remember, referees don't win or lose basketball games. Missed layups and missed free throws lose basketball games.

Note that the longer you coach, the more often you will encounter the same referees. It doesn't pay to be their antagonist. There will be games where the team can't get a call or break. This can be stressful for the players and the coach, so again, it's key to keep things positive. Tell the players to ignore the calls and keep battling. The more they worry about the referees, the worse they will play. It's critical to focus on your team's performance, not the referee's. Don't ever make the referee a scapegoat for losing a game.

Helping Players Do Their Best

Basketball is not an easy game to master. Players will make mistakes, lots of them, and coaches must resist the temptation to enumerate each of them to a player's face. Doing so repeatedly can be discouraging at best, and devastating at worst. So keep it light, and keep it positive.

It's important that every individual critique be handled in private, out of earshot of the rest of the team. Correcting a player is not the same as criticizing the player. Think of it as teaching, not criticizing. The player will always be more receptive to being taught if the criticism is folded inside a compliment, preferably two. Start with a positive, make the teaching point, and then finish with another positive.

For example, you could say, *I love the way you hustled at the game yesterday. Just make sure to square up your shoulders to the basket when you shoot. I know if you do that, you're going to score a lot of points.* That's called positive reinforcement.

This approach inspires, rather than deflates. It instills in players a love of the game and a desire to improve. It's the first step toward turning a great game into an ongoing life lesson about the merits of working hard and working with teammates to overcome obstacles and achieve goals. It's the first step toward turning an eager kid into a basketball player, and an eager adult into a basketball coach.

The Coach's Clipboard

✔ A coach has the most influence in practice; in games, it's primarily up to the kids.

✔ Hissy fits don't work. Patient repetition of key points does.

✔ Keep the shouting of instructions during a game to a minimum.

✔ Keep it simple and brief during time-outs: Offer one or two instructions about specific actions.

✔ Review plays before the game on the dry-erase board.

✔ Remind the players that when you talk, no one else should; open the floor to questions after you're done.

✔ Emphasize effort, hustle, and teamwork. Scoring and winning are bonuses.

✔ Don't expect your players to do something in a game that they can't pull off in a practice.

✔ Keep track of playing time and rotate players in and out of the game to keep everyone involved.

✔ Emphasize respect for the game, the opponent, and the referees.

✔ Strive to inspire.

# About the Authors

With 19 years of youth basketball coaching experience and 8 years of coaching high school, Coach **Keith Miniscalco** knows how to develop youth players to excel at all levels. He has coached both boys and girls in several acclaimed Chicago park district and youth school leagues, including Our Lady of Lourdes and Queen of All Saints grade schools, Loyola Academy High School, and his own highly respected Over the Edge youth basketball travel program. He cofounded and currently runs Over the Edge in Chicago (overtheedgehoops.com). The program's goal is to prepare youth-level players for high school competition. It has seen great success and has proven to be extremely effective for young athletes who wish to continue with competitive basketball. Coach Miniscalco lives in Chicago.

A full-time music critic for the *Chicago Tribune*, **Greg Kot** fills much of his spare time coaching with Miniscalco in their Over the Edge program for youth basketball players. An accomplished writer, Kot has been the *Chicago Tribune*'s pop critic since 1990. He is a regular contributor to numerous national publications, including *Rolling Stone*, and cohosts the nationally syndicated radio show *Sound Opinions* on public radio. He authored the acclaimed rock biography *Wilco: Learning How to Die* in 2004 for Broadway Books, and his next book, *Ripped: How the Wired Generation Revolutionized Music*, will be published by Scribner in 2009. Kot lives in Chicago.